Biology and Social Behavior

Allan Mazur
Leon S. Robertson

Biology
and
Social Behavior

The Free Press, New York
Collier-Macmillan, Limited, London

To Nancy and Polly

The Free Press
A Division of The Macmillan Company
866 Third Avenue, New York, New York 10022

Collier-Macmillan Canada Ltd., Toronto, Ontario

Library of Congress Catalog Card Number: 72–169236

printing number
1 2 3 4 5 6 7 8 9 10

PREFACE

MANY READERS WILL BEGIN THIS BOOK WITH
the belief that men are biologically-driven beasts, and many
others will begin it thinking that biological theorizing is racist.
We should say at the outset that the book follows neither of those
positions. We will discuss the interaction of biological, psychological and social factors in human behavior.

Though we don't write as well as Mark Twain, we have tried
for a "Huckleberry Finn effect," that is, to appeal to a broad audience, from professional social scientists to the general reader. An
extensive background in biology is not required.

The book is organized into three main parts, and these are
bracketed by a first and a last chapter appropriately titled
"Introduction" and "Conclusion." In the absence of a unifying
theory of biological factors in social behavior, we have planned
the parts around three broad methodological strategies: interspecies comparisons, intraspecies comparisons, and biological
manipulations.

This short treatment omits a great deal of relevant biology.
Perhaps the most debatable of these omissions is neurobiology,
which some behaviorists would argue to be central to our topic.
The interested reader is referred to Quarton, et al (1967), C. Smith
(1970), and Schmitt, et al (1970) for good summaries of this
literature.

We appreciate the criticism and advice of Patricia Barchas,
R. Allen Gardner and B. T. Gardner, Jay and Suzanne Mitten-
thal, Stephen Richer, Dale Rolfsen, and particularly Theodore

Melnechuck of the Neurosciences Research Project at M.I.T. We are grateful to Robert B. Smith, who suggested that we do the book.

A.M.
L.S.R.

CONTENTS

CHAPTER 1   INTRODUCTION:

WE ARE KILLERS BY NATURE, AND THEREIN lies the problem of war and peace: how to soothe the savage beast. This theme runs through recent best sellers devoted to some biological bases of human behavior: *African Genesis* (Ardrey, 1961), *The Territorial Imperative* (Ardrey, 1966), *On Aggression* (Lorenz, 1966), *The Naked Ape* (Morris, 1967), and *Men in Groups* (Tiger, 1969). They vary in credibility, but all are provocative and have hooked the public imagination.

The major response of those few social scientists who have chosen to react to these books has been to derogate them for ignoring the learned cultural basis of human behavior (e.g., Montagu, 1968b). One best seller dismisses culture in the first chapter, arguing:

> If the organization of our earthier activities—our feeding, our fear, our aggression, our sex, our parental care—had been developed solely by cultural means, there can be little doubt that we would have got it under better control by now, and twisted it this way and that to suit the increasingly extraordinary demands put upon it by our technological advances (Morris, 1967:34).[1]

As if we had the *cultural* problems of society "under better control by now." It is partly because of this sort of argument that social scientists disdain the best sellers, and even the better ones (such as Lorenz's *On Aggression*) suffer from negative halo effect. In spite of their popular impact, the biological notions in these

[1] From *The Naked Ape* by Desmond Morris. Copyright © 1967 by Desmond Morris. Used with permission of McGraw-Hill Book Company.

1

works are more often ignored than confronted by the social sciences.

Social science textbook writers often devote a few paragraphs to the "nature-nurture issue," and some conclude that nature and nurture "interact" in the development of human beings and their social behavior, but details of the interaction are usually not presented. A number of biologists, psychologists, ethologists, and anthropologists and a few sociologists have maintained an interest in biological factors in human behavior, and new data are accumulating. But they are only beginning to have an impact on contemporary social science.

If biological and social phenomena do interact in their effects on social behavior, we may ask why social scientists have been reluctant to become involved in what appears to be a field ripe for investigation. Three social scientists have recently called their fellows' attention to this reluctance and suggested a number of reasons for the neglect (Clausen, 1967; Eckland, 1967; Means, 1967).

Eckland (1967) attributes social science's neglect of genetics to such factors as "vested interest in establishing a strong environmentalist approach," cultural anthropologists' thinking that biological evolution of man has ended and has been replaced by cultural evolution, and ideology which holds that all men should be treated as equal. Clausen (1967) notes similar factors in his citation of social scientists' aversion to reductionism [2] and racism. Means (1967) adds their overreaction to poor theory and methodology in research showing relationships between gross morphology (race, "somatypes," [3] etc.) and behavior.

This was not always the case. Although much theorizing about society and social behavior occurred throughout recorded history, the formation of social science disciplines separate from theology and philosophy came about in the latter half of the nineteenth century. Darwin's theory of evolution was the "great discovery" of the day, and the first men to call themselves social scientists were profoundly influenced by it.[4]

---

[2] Reductionism refers to the notion that sociological principles can be derived from psychological principles, psychological principles from biological principles, and so on.

[3] Kretschmer (1925) in Germany and Sheldon (cf 1940) in the United States developed somewhat similar theories that temperament, mental disease, delinquency, etc. were related to body form or "somatype." Chapter 7 contains a brief discussion of somatypes.

[4] Social scientists were not alone in this regard. See, for example, Grinker (1967) for an account of the rise and fall of "genetic psychology."

For example, Herbert Spencer thought of society as analogous to an organism,[5] and Darwin's theory gave impetus to the notion. Soon people were being thought of as analogous to cells, groups to organs, nervous systems to communication, or societies to evolving species. (Martindale, 1960; Becker and Barnes, 1961). Some early theorists took the philosophical and theological position that mind and body are separate entities and that social science should be constructed on psychological rather than biological principles (Ward, 1895). However, others defended the position that "all sociological manifestations proceed from physiological conditions" (Thomas, 1897).

Had the debate remained purely scientific, new evidence and better logic might have resulted in an integrated theory of bio-psycho-social factors in man's behavior. However, current "knowledge" often is taken as a reason or justification for action, and "scientific" theories are often used to justify the social order or the development of a new order. For example, William Graham Sumner, the noted American sociologist, was a "Social Darwinist" who thought that social classes evolved because of the advancement if not the survival of the fittest—particularly the industrial "robber barons" of the late nineteenth century—and justified the perpetuation of inequalities on that basis.

And, of course, there is race. In America, slavery was often justified by assumptions of racial inferiority (Ruchames, 1969). In Europe, in the mid-1800s, Arthur de Gobineau proposed a racial theory of human history which held that the black and yellow peoples of the world had never developed a civilization and that, among the whites, the "nordic" group showed "the greatest capacity for creative civilization." H. S. Chamberlain, an Englishman who claimed "nordic" ancestry and became a German citizen, popularized the notion in a book, *Foundations of the Nineteenth Century,* which was used in Germany as "a sort of Nordic bible" (Ellwood, 1938).

These notions were not just a part of popular mythology; they pervaded the scientific community as well. The *American Journal of Sociology* contained up until the mid-1930s (at which time it was the official journal of the American Sociological Society) a number of articles which either attempted to prove or

---

[5] Reasoning by analogy may be valuable for generating hypotheses, but to assume that one set of phenomena which superficially appear to behave like another set of phenomena are doing so because of the same processes often leads to false conclusions. This is one of the problems of generalizing from animal to human behavior or among species of animals.

assumed superiority-inferiority of peoples on the basis of one or another concept of race. For example, Clossen (1897) attempted to show the superiority of "Homo Europoeus" (nordic) over "Homo Alpinus" and the Mediterranean "races" in terms of the wealth, taxes, etc. found in different areas of Europe. Park (1931), in an article on "Mentality of Racial Hybrids," assumed that dark-skinned persons were inferior. Ross (1924) justified immigration quotas on the basis of similar assumptions.

Whether or not the purging of racism from sociological theories resulted from new knowledge of race gained by biologists and physical anthropologists and knowledge of culture and civilization gained by sociologists, cultural anthropologists, and historians, we cannot say. No doubt they were influential, but we suspect that revulsion to Hitler's use of racist theories to justify genocide had as much to do with it as anything else. Reviewing Hitler's theories of race and the "joys" of human struggle, Opler (1945) wrote "There is not room on one small planet for the atomic bomb and groups of mankind who fancy they are playing the role of Darwin's barnacles."

Our purpose in pointing out these trends is not to scoff at our intellectual predecessors and certainly not to lament the loss of racist theorizing. It is merely to offer possible reasons for the present state of social science theories regarding biological factors in social behavior. It also raises unresolved questions regarding the degree to which objective theories of social behavior can be constructed given the values of social scientists and of the societies in which they live.

Is it in the interest of social scientists to maintain an "environmentalist approach?" If they are to have credibility in the long run, we think not. The credible scientist builds theories which are accurate predictors of the phenomena in question. To ignore a possible major contributing factor may result in a theory which is not predictive. To ignore biological contributions to behavior because of the mistakes of the past is foolish. For scientists, political leaders, or others to infer that people should live or die or have special privileges on the basis of such criteria, or any criteria, is to make a value or politically calculated judgment, not to state a scientific conclusion.

The issue of reductionism is a matter for empirical research. Whether or not principles regarding cultural, political, or other social phenomena can be reduced to psychological or biological principles is not a question of values but a hypothesis to be investigated. Assume for a moment that such reduction were possible: Would social science be dismantled? Undoubtedly it would not. Chemistry can largely be reduced to physics but it would be extremely inefficient to investigate or state all chemical principles in terms of the laws of physics. As sociological "equations" are developed, their terms will probably include biological and psychological elements, but surely they will include uniquely sociological terms as well. Those who take into account additional factors which might contribute to the phenomena they are investigating will be in a better position to make the major discoveries in the coming years. It is the purpose of this book to call attention to some findings and methodological strategies which we think will be important in this process.

PART I

Differences Among Species

A behavior *may be just as intrinsic to an animal species as a* physical *feature. In fact, behavioral characteristics are sometimes used to differentiate closely related species which look alike.*

Humans presumably have intrinsic behavioral characteristics, like all other animals. Such a behavior would occur in any human society—even a society that was fully isolated from contact with other societies.

Archeologists are continually finding that there was more communication between prehistoric communities than previously thought, and so we can never ignore the possibility that cross-cultural similarities in behavior and social institutions (e.g., incest tabus) are the result of cultural diffusion. Since this highly feasible explanation can rarely be discounted, it is difficult to show that any given behavior is intrinsically human in the sense that it would be expected to occur even in a society that had been isolated from culture contact. The task is not impossible, however, and we will attempt it here.

Our method will be analogous to the method of comparative anatomy which generates hypotheses about the evolution of physical characteristics by comparing closely related species. We will look for ordered progression of social characteristics across closely related primate species. If such behaviors do occur in an ordered sequence, and they extend to man, then it seems reasonable to consider them human species characteristics rather than effects of cultural diffusion.

7

CHAPTER 2

SOCIAL BEHAVIOR
AMONG PRIMATES

IN MOVING UP THE PHYLOGENETIC TREE
from protozoa through chordates, vertebrates, mammals, and
primates to man, it is clear that there is a progression not only
in biological structure but also in behavior. The importance of
learned behavior and the tendency to form social aggregates both
increase; social groups become stratified by a dominance order;
there is increased dependence on adults for nurturance and
training of young; and affectional systems develop.

We make no inference about the goodness or superiority of
a "higher" species over a "lower" species.[1] We are simply concerned here with noting that there is a reasonable biological
ordering of species which places man at one end and which also
orders many aspects of *species behavior* in such a way that there
is a clear progression toward human behavior. Our aim is to
use such an ordering to better understand human social behavior.

A BIOLOGICAL SERIES OF PRIMATES

This chapter will be concerned only with those species closest
in biological structure to man. We will focus on the primates, that
order which includes man, apes, monkeys, and prosimians.
Strictly speaking, living species cannot generally be arranged in

---

[1] If being a bug is the thing you do, who is to say that being a rabbit
is any better?

a phylogenetic tree since each living species is the termination of its own branch. Yet:

> It is often possible to arrange (living) members of a common group in a graded series which strongly suggests an actual scale of evolutionary development. For example, in the Primates . . . such a series may be constructed by comparing, in order, Man, chimpanzees, monkeys, tarsier, lemur and tree-shrew. . . . Here . . . we seem to have a number of graded links through which the bodily structure of Man is connected with that of small mammals of quite a lowly appearance. . . . What a series of this kind does indicate is that, apart altogether from extinct fossil forms, there are connecting links *of an approximate kind* between Man and the lower mammals . . . (Clark, 1961:9–10).

The biological series (2–1) furnished by Clark will be used with some modification. The group "monkeys" will be subdivided into "higher monkeys," represented here by the closely related genera of baboons and macaques, and "lower monkeys," represented by New World squirrel monkeys.[2] This leaves the following series in which there is a progression in at least some biological structures: tree-shrew, lemur, tarsier, squirrel monkey, baboon and macaque, chimp, man. Figure 2–2 illustrates, for example, graded changes in the brains of these primates.[3] Due to lack of behavioral information on tree-shrews and tarsiers, the treatment below will be limited to the lemur, squirrel monkey, baboon and macaque, chimp, and man.

We are concerned with using such a biological series for a comparative study of social behavior. A helpful basic assumption is that the social behavior of human and nonhuman primates differs largely in degree, rather than totally in kind. In view of the recent work on primate societies (e.g., Southwick, 1963; De Vore, 1965; Jay, 1968), this sort of assumption should be acceptable to social science. There can no longer be serious claims that mother love, norms, social control, community loyalty, and even tool-making culture, are purely human.

---

[2] These particular genera have been selected because they have been relatively well studied and because we are personally most familiar with them. Our designation of the squirrel monkey as a "lower monkey" relative to the baboon and macaque is justified on the basis of biological structure. On this same basis, squirrel monkeys have been called "half-monkeys" (Sanderson, 1957:68).

[3] Recent renewal of interest in comparative neurology of these species (Noback and Montagna, 1970) may lead to specification of the biological elements which explain some of the behavioral differences noted in this chapter.

FIGURE 2–1. The primate series.

a. Treeshrew .(*Tupaia glis belangeri;* San Diego Zoo photo).

b. Lemur (*Lemur catta;* San Diego Zoo photo by Ron Garrison).

c. Tarsier (*Tarsius syrichta carbonarius;* San Diego Zoo photo by Ron Garrison).

d. Squirrel monkey (*Saimiri sciureus;* San Diego Zoo photo by Ron Garrison).

e. Macaque (*Macaca sylvana;* San Diego Zoo photo).

f. Chimpanzee (*Pan troglodytes;* San Diego Zoo photo by Ron Garrison).

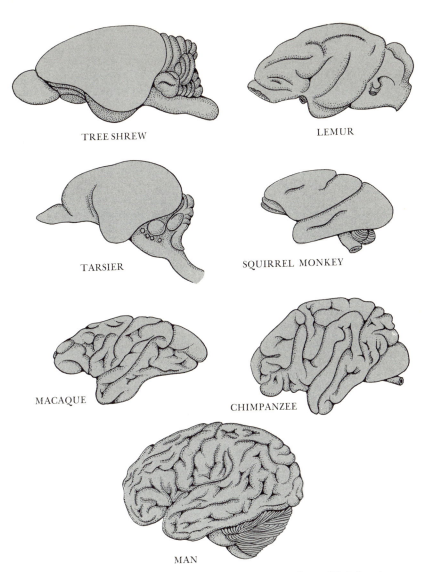

TREE SHREW

LEMUR

TARSIER

SQUIRREL MONKEY

MACAQUE

CHIMPANZEE

MAN

FIGURE 2–2. Brains of primates. Side views of tree shrew (*Tupaia minor;* Le Gros Clark, 1959: 237), lemur (*Lemur catta;* Le Gros Clark, 1959: 246), tarsier (*Tarsius spectrum;* Le Gros Clark, 1959: 251), squirrel monkey (*Saimiri sciurea;* Hill, 1960: 287), macaque (Napier and Napier, 1967: 28), chimpanzee (*Pan satyrus;* Hill, 1955: 73), and man (Napier and Napier, 1967: 28). Not drawn to uniform scale.

PROGRESSION IN SOCIAL BEHAVIOR

Our next step is to argue that, as we examine the forms of social behavior of each of the primates in the biological series, moving from lemur to man, these forms of social behavior progressively become more similar to human social behavior. Consider juvenile play behavior:

The play behavior of chimpanzee and man is remarkably more complex than that of monkey, with man being the most manipulative and object oriented of all primates in his play. Surely it is more than a coincidence that the nonhuman primate taxonomically closest to man (i.e., the chimp) . . . is also the most manipulative, exploratory, and similar to man in play. The range of variation in play form and games among chimpanzees is second only to man. . . .

When contrasted with chimpanzee play, in which object manipulation is a major feature, monkey play involves predominantly locomotor patterns such as wrestling and chasing with other young. . . .

Little, if any, attention is directed to play with objects or to manipulation of many items in the environment (Jay, 1968:501–502).

Field observations of young squirrel monkeys [4] support Jay's characterization of monkey play as mainly locomotor (lots of wrestling and chasing) with very little object manipulation. Wild lemurs almost never manipulate objects during play (or at any other time), and their games are relatively inactive:

The rough-and-tumble chases of young baboons look frenetically active compared with *Propithecus* (a lemur species) play. The effect comes from the slow-motion, almost stylized fumbling (of the lemurs) for each other (Jolly, 1966:59).

Not only is there increasing richness of play as we move up the primate series but also increasingly long infancy and juvenile periods during which the young animal learns appropriate social behavior.[5]

---

[4] Mazur and John Baldwin conducted these field observations during a three-month period at Monkey Jungle, Florida, in the summer of 1966. Monkey Jungle has large, well-established societies of semi-free-ranging squirrel monkeys and crab-eating macaques. DuMond (1967) provides a fuller description of Monkey Jungle.

[5] The lemur takes 2 to 3 years to become adult; the squirrel monkey takes about 3 to 6 years; baboons and macaques probably take 5 to 8 years; chimps about 12 years; and human beings from 16 to 21 years (Jolly, 1966,; Baldwin, 1969; Hall and DeVore, 1965; Koford, 1963; Van Lawick-Goodall, 1968).

That an animal practices in play the skills and activities he needs when grown is of tremendous evolutionary importance. Infant and juvenile stages of development last much longer in the chimpanzee than similar phases do in monkeys, and it is reasonable to suppose that the chimpanzee has correspondingly more to learn. This supposition is supported by the richness of adult chimpanzee social behavior when compared with that of any monkey . . . (Jay, 1968:501).

Adult social behavior as manifested in, for example, adult face-to-face interaction varies greatly in amount and quality across the primate series. Chimpanzee interaction can take place between any age-sex classes, just as in human society. Chimps use a wide range of expressive calls, gestures, and postures, some of which are similar to those made by man (Van Lawick-Goodall, 1968). Within baboon and macaque troops there is also much face-to-face interaction, but it seems to be more rigidly structured along age, sex, and dominance lines. Also, there apparently is less range of expressive behaviors. One of us (Mazur) has personally compared interactional behavior of semi-free-ranging societies of squirrel monkeys and macaques, and the differences are immediately apparent. Adult squirrel monkeys show relatively little face-to-face interaction outside of seasonal sexual behavior, and "aunting" behavior between adult females and an infant (Baldwin, 1969). Their main social activity is the maintenance of a contiguous spacing during the day and a huddling together in small sleeping groups at night. The squirrel monkey's range of expressive actions seems much more limited than that of the macaque. The lemur, at the end of the primate series, shows relatively little face-to-face interaction beyond huddling in contact (Petter, 1965: 309–310; Jolly, 1966:55–58).

A completely different aspect of social behavior which progresses along the primate series is the tendency for copulatory behavior to move from short, well-defined mating periods to the year-round mating found in human beings. The lemur breeding season is extremely short, apparently less than two weeks (Jolly, 1966:156). Squirrel monkeys have a breeding season of two or three months (DuMond and Hutchinson, 1967). Rhesus macaque mating occurs mainly during a three-month period, but some copulation occurs during about half the year; chimpanzee mating is nonseasonal, according to Washburn and Hamburg (1965:610).

Another aspect of societal behavior which seems to correlate with the primate biological series is the incidence of a technological culture. Not only do chimpanzees *use* simple tools (e.g., they pry with sticks, throw stones, wipe themselves with leaves), but they also *make* them. Chimps will chew up leaves in order to make effective sponges. They will select twigs and trim them to appropriate size for use in catching termites [6] (Goodall, 1965; Jay, 1968:496).

If man and chimp have technological cultures, according to the primate series baboons and macaques should be the next most likely candidates to show some such technology. Although at this time there is no known tool making among either of these animals, the following technology has been reported in one troop of Japanese macaques:

Perhaps the most striking invention by the troop on Koshima has to do with the eating of wheat. Picking up the wheat scattered on the beach proved to be rather tiresome work, the more so since sand almost inevitably got mixed with the food. A solution to this problem has been found: the monkeys carry the wheat to the sea and plunge it into the water; the sand falls to the bottom of the water thus separating from the wheat, making it easy to eat the remaining and purified wheat. The workers of the Japan Monkey Center insist that this method of sifting the sand from the wheat has never been taught or shown to the monkeys (Frisch, 1968:249–251).

No comparable technology has been even hinted at in squirrel monkeys, although they have not been observed so thoroughly as macaques. Mazur has seen squirrel monkeys occasionally handle bits of wood or leaves but has never observed anything approaching tool use. Lemurs in the wild have very little tendency to handle any inanimate objects other than food (Jolly, 1966:78).

There are indications that the family bond [7] exists among chimpanzees. The chimp offspring maintain fairly close contact with their mothers at least into adolescence (about age eight). After an offspring has ceased to depend on its mother for food, transportation, and protection, the bond is still shown by preferential grooming behavior, tolerance during feeding, and mutual

---

[6] The chimp inserts the stripped and trimmed twig into a crevice containing termites. The termites walk up the twig, and the chimp then licks them off. It is interesting that 40 years before Goodall observed this behavior in wild chimps, Köhler observed captive chimps using straws to catch ants in essentially the same manner (Köhler, 1927:76–77).

[7] Family bonding among nonhuman primates does not generally include anything analogous to monogamy (an exception is the gibbon which is monogamous). However, monogamy is not a general characteristic of human beings either. Consider that in the United States 25 percent of all marriages end in divorce (Lang, 1969:72).

defense. A mother and her independent son will coalesce if one is attacked by a family outsider (Van Lawick-Goodall, 1967a:316–318). Older siblings have been observed to show maternal care for a younger sibling. On one occasion, after the death of the mother, an older sib essentially adopted the younger, letting him sleep with her at night, protecting him, and waiting for him when she moved about (Van Lawick-Goodall, 1967b:186).

Macaques also show some of these indicators of familial bond. The incidence of sitting together and grooming is relatively high between mother and offspring, and there is a high degree of mutual tolerance at food hoppers. These relations exist into adulthood. Also, an offspring's rank in the social dominance order is at least partly determined by its mother's rank (Reynolds, 1968; Sade, 1967). These observations can be made only over a number of years when the group's genealogy is known. In the next few years we should have much better data on the status of family relationships in chimps and macaques, and we hope there will be some comparable data on the lower primates.

Our tentative conclusion on the basis of the evidence presented here is that the biologically progressing primate series may also be considered a behaviorally progressing series. It appears that we can follow orderly changes in social behavior from lemur to man and infer that each level of social behavior is in some sense intrinsic to each species. One additional aspect of social behavior will be considered below as a further demonstration of this point.

DOMINANCE AND SOCIAL CONTROL

Recent field studies show a fairly consistent picture of dominance and social control in baboon and macaque societies (Imanishi, 1963; Washburn and DeVore, 1963; Koford, 1963; Hall and DeVore, 1965; Southwick, Beg, and Siddiqi, 1965; Simonds, 1965). Social control is based on a recognized male dominance hierarchy. This dominance order is not necessarily linear, and animals acting in coalition may improve their status, but the order is sufficiently clear so that troop leaders can easily be differentiated from non-leaders. Factors associated with a dominant status are priority to food and resting places, aggressive gestures toward less dominant troop members (but rarely physical attack), and receipt of submissive gestures from the less dominant. When food is thrown between two individuals, both behave as if it belongs to the more dominant. The dominant individual will take the food while the submissive individual averts his eyes and does not even try for it. This sort of dominance behavior is evidently based on a well-developed normative system, and we may think of it as a *deference* structure equally as well as a *dominance* structure. The most dominant male is the troop leader. He is in the forefront during intertroop combat or in defense against a predator. When a dispute breaks out between troop members, the leader will usually stop it with a threat. He will give immediate protection to any mother with an infant who is threatened by another animal.

The leader and the deference-dominance structure of baboon and macaque societies form a very effective system of social control which is similar to status and social control mechanisms in human groups.[8] The main difference is that the baboon and macaque systems are very much dependent on overt gestures of threat and submissiveness, whereas human groups usually depend on more subtle interactions to enforce status rankings and social conformity. Apparently, as we move up the primate series, means of controlling status and conformity become less overt and more subtle. Chimpanzee dominance and social control fit into this pattern (Nishida, 1970). There are relatively few overt aggressive or submissive gestures. Interactions are more subtle and have made it difficult for human observers to ascertain dominance ordering.

However, when regular observations became possible on the interactions between the various individuals it gradually became evident that the social status of each chimpanzee was fairly well defined in relation to each other individual. In other words, it was often possible to predict, when for example two chimpanzees met on a narrow branch, which animal would gain the right of way; that animal could then be described as the dominant one of the two (Van Lawick-Goodall, 1968:315).

As we move *down* the primate series, from baboons and macaques to squirrel monkeys and lemurs, the highly normative regulation of status and conformity gives way to a system where dominance and control are enforced on the weaker by the stronger. We have already mentioned that semi-free-ranging squirrel monkeys are relatively noninteractive outside mating season, and so

[8] Barchas and Fisek (1969) have compared status formation and maintenance in three-man ad hoc groups of college freshmen and rhesus macaques. Although there were some species differences, in general the status process seems to be similar for both groups.

it is difficult to evaluate their dominance behaviors during most of the year. Therefore our data on these behaviors come from confined colonies in which the animals were more interactive because of their close contact. In this situation, Ploog and MacLean (1963) report that dominance interactions were frequently characterized by chase, physical assault, and stylized penile display by the more dominant animal. Mazur's observations of a newly formed colony of 10 adults (4 males and 6 females) confirmed the importance of agonistic "hands-on" behavior by the more dominant animal, as opposed to deferent behavior by the less dominant animal. One could determine a strict linear dominance order very quickly by placing food between two individuals and noting which individual ended up with it. But the nature of these interactions was very different than is found among baboons and macaques. There the less dominant animal would avert his gaze and not even try for the food. Here both animals would reach for it, and the more dominant squirrel monkey would consistently end up with it only because he took it from the less dominant one. There was no hint of any deference behavior.[9]

The lemur, at the bottom of the primate series, seems similar to the squirrel monkey in that dominance order is not easily observable since there is relatively little interaction. As with squirrel monkeys, the lemur handles dominance relations with "hands on" power tactics rather than with deference norms. In most spats where two animals come in contact, one lemur swats with one or sometimes alternate hands toward the other's face (Jolly, 1966:99).

It is significant that [lemur] aggressive interactions . . . seemed to take place between individuals, with no tendency to defend the underdog in a spat and with no central hierarchy of males who mutually defended each other, as in many baboon and rhesus [macaque] troops . . . Neither . . . [was] "protected threat" [observed], that is, when one animal avoided the attack of a dominant by standing near another still more dominant (Jolly, 1966:110).

It seems reasonable to hypothesize that, as we move up the primate series, dominance-control systems become characterized less by overt "hands on" power behavior and more by subtle,

---

[9] It is possible that the squirrel monkeys' rough physical interaction was a result of their caged confinement. However, P. Barchas (personal communication) has studied dominance behavior in caged rhesus macaques, and she reports that under her conditions there is minimal agonistic physical contact.

normatively based deference-dominance behavior. The final stage of this trend appears in man: status and control in face-to-face groups is generally quite subtle, and physical agonistic attack within the group is rare. Our almost complete dependence on norms rather than "hands on" power to regulate status and conformity in face-to-face groups may be the basis for the notion of "legitimacy" in the political control of larger human aggregates.

TARSIERS

The theory which we have suggested here can be tested directly. As we noted at the beginning of this chapter, the tarsier fits into the biological primate series between lemur and squirrel monkey; therefore, if the tarsier is viewed in the context of the series, as in Table 2–1, it is a straightforward matter to deduce several aspects of tarsier social behavior. We would predict that the play of tarsier young will be almost purely locomotor with little object manipulation; it will take about three years for a tarsier to reach adulthood (see footnote 5); adults will be relatively noninteractive and will have a limited range of expressive gestures; there will be a fairly short and well-defined breeding season; there will be no sign of tool using; and tarsier dominance and social control will depend on overt "hands on" agonistic power behavior rather than on subtle normative behavior. The confirmation or denial of these predictions will have to await field studies of tarsier society.

TERRITORY

The primate series has interesting applications. For example, there has been recent conjecture that much human social organization is based on a territorial instinct. Certain birds, fish, and mammals instinctively take over and defend plots of ground with fairly specific boundaries (Lorenz, 1966). Perhaps the best evidence of this behavior is the stylized territorial boundary "marking" of some mammals with urine or special glandular secretions, although this sort of marking is evidently used in other contexts as well (Ralls, 1971). Some writers argue that this instinctive behavior (without the marking) extends to man, and that it can account for his warlike tendencies (Ardrey, 1966). If this is true, the territorial instinct should be a consistent aspect of the primate series.

Some lemurs clearly show territorial defense, including marking (Jolly, 1966). Tree shrews, who are even lower on the primate series, have throat and chest glands which are used for marking (Marler, 1965:548), although it is not clear that this has territorial significance. There are some indications of territorial instinct and/or marking behavior in titis monkeys (W. Mason, 1968) and tamarins (Mazur and Baldwin, 1968). Although these last two primates have not been included in the primate series used here, on biological grounds they would probably fit near squirrel monkeys (see footnote 11). Much study of baboons, macaques, and chimps shows no sign of territorial instinct, with or without marking. These troops do live on fairly well-defined home ranges, and they do sometimes have agonistic interactions with neighboring troops, but there is no evidence that they are defending a territory per se; they simply defend the spot they occupy at the moment (Carpenter, 1965; Washburn and Hamburg, 1965). There is no observed tendency to defend regular boundaries, and in fact the boundaries of neighboring ranges usually overlap. The trend which appears in the primate series is that the importance of territorial instinct *declines* as we move toward man. There seems to be no biological basis for considering territoriality to be an important factor in human social behavior.

There is one striking anomaly in the trend: The gibbon, who fits biologically into the series *above* baboons and macaques, does show signs of a territorial instinct.

If the intergroup encounters among rhesus (macaques) . . . are compared with those of *H. lar* (i.e., gibbons) it is obvious that the rhesus monkeys are not programmed phylogenetically for efficient territoriality; conversely, gibbons have evolved an elaborate behavioral complex for dealing with frequent intergroup encounters. There are built-in mechanisms that allow gibbon groups . . . to go through protracted territorial ceremonies (Ellefson, 1968:198).

Gibbons are anomalous among primates in many respects. Their universal monogamy and lack of juvenile peer and play groups are oddities among the higher primates. "Gibbons occupy a unique position among nonhuman primates. They are the smallest, by a factor of ten, of the anthropoid apes; they are probably the most primitive and yet by far the most successful of the apes in number and distribution" (Ellefson, 1968:180). At present we cannot explain this anomaly.

Table 2-1 Behavior progression along the primate series.

Behavior	Primate							
	Tree shrew	Lemur	Tarsier	Squirrel monkey	Baboon and macaque	Chimp	Proto-man	Man
Juvenile play		Stylized locomotor; no object manipulation		Predominantly locomotor; little object manipulation	Predominantly locomotor; little object manipulation	Complex games; high object manipulation		Most complex games; highest object manipulation
Pre-adult socialization period (in yrs.)		2–3		3–6	5–8	~12		16–21
Adult face-to-face interaction		Little interaction beyond huddling; few types of expressive gestures		Little adult interaction other than mating and "aunting"; few types of expressive gestures	High interaction but rigidly structured along age, sex, and dominance lines; many types of expressive gestures	High interaction between any age-sex classes; many types of expressive gestures		Most interaction between any age-sex classes; most types of expressive gestures
Mating periodicity		2-week season		2–3-month season	Mainly during 3-month season, but also out of season	Nonseasonal		Nonseasonal

	None; no object manipulation	None; little object manipulation	Simple problem solving	Simple tool use and tool making	Complex tool making
Technological culture	None; no object manipulation	None; little object manipulation	Simple problem solving	Simple tool use and tool making	Complex tool making
Family bond			Some sign of bond in macaques	Signs of long-term bond	Highest degree of family bond
Dominance and social control	No sign of deference; no sign of group social control; "hands on" agonistic behavior	No sign of deference; no sign of social control; stylized dominance display; "hands on" agonistic behavior	Dominance-deference ordering; social control maintained by leader; overt threat and dominance gestures; little "hands on" agonistic behavior	Dominance-deference ordering; subtle threat and dominance gestures; little "hands on" agonistic behavior	Highest degree of stratification and social control; most subtle threat and dominance gestures; little "hands on" agnostic behavior
Territorial behavior — Marking glands	Territory defense, including marking	Urine display	None	None	

PROTO-HUMAN BEHAVIOR

If the behavior of tarsiers can be inferred by fitting them into the primate series, perhaps we can do the same for the extinct genera of proto-humans—Australopithecus, Pithecanthropus, and Neanderthal man. In our series they all fit between chimps and modern man. Therefore, we would expect the young of these "men" to have had complex play games with much object manipulation; they would have taken 12 to 16 years to reach adulthood (see footnote 5). Adults were highly interactive, using many of the expressive gestures we retain today. They copulated without regard to season, and they had a tool-using and tool-making culture.[10] Furthermore, they had a well-developed social-stratification and social-control system based on generally accepted norms, and there was no bonking each other on the head with clubs in order to get what they wanted. They were not motivated by a territorial instinct. In sum, they may have been much more like modern man than is commonly thought.

FUTURE WORK

If the series approach to comparative sociology looks promising, its pursuit involves several research chores. First, more data are needed on different species in order to evaluate, correct, and refine the trends which have been indicated here. At the least, data on tarsiers are necessary. Second, some standard form of data collection and analysis should be developed which would facilitate cross-species comparisons without forcing field workers into an overly rigid research framework. Third, many more than the new social behaviors considered here must be traced through the primate series.

Finally some problems of explanation must be resolved. Relatively complex social organization is found among bees (Chapter 3) and other insects far removed from man in the phylogenetic tree. If we tried to add these social insects to our series, we would find the most complex social organization at opposite ends of the biological order. It is clear that the biological-behavioral progression of species is not linear once we leave the primates. Even

---

[10] There is already good archeological evidence of tool-making cultures among these early proto-humans (Dart, 1959; Brace, 1967).

within the order of primates there is nonlinearity (e.g., the gibbon), and perhaps there are more than one primate series. As soon as data are available the primates should be divided into separate Old World and New World series.[11]

The mechanisms whereby behavior progresses across the series is not known. It would be fallacious to conclude that each of these behaviors is "wired in" to each species. Perhaps some behaviors in the progression are explained by increasing ability to learn very "obvious" forms of social interaction and increasing capacity for culture. Whatever the mechanisms, these progressive behaviors are species characteristics in the same sense that physical features are species specific.

Suggested Reading

Two good collections of field studies of primate social behavior are *Primate Behavior,* edited by I. DeVore (Holt, Rinehart and Winston; New York: 1965); and *Primates: Studies in Adaptation and Variability,* edited by P. Jay (Holt, Rinehart and Winston; New York: 1968).

The Antecedents of Man, by W. Le Gros Clark (Edinburgh University Press; Edinburgh: 1957) contains a detailed discussion of the comparative anatomy of primates.

The Life of Primates, by A. Schultz (Universe Books; New York: 1969) surveys the various types of living primates, providing general descriptions of biological differences, habitat, and behavior.

Perspectives on Human Evolution, edited by S. Washburn and P. Jay (Holt, Rinehart and Winston; New York: 1968) discusses the physical and behavioral characteristics of man from (as the name implies) an evolutionary perspective.

---

[11] An expanded biological series for the Old World might be: tupaioids (tree shrews); lemurs; tarsiers; cercopithecoids (swamp monkeys, guenons, red monkeys); cynopithecoids (mangabeys, macaques, baboons); apes (chimps, gorillas, orangutans, gibbons); and man. A tentative New World series might be: hapaloids (marmosets, tamarins, titis); pithecoids (ucaris, sakis, squirrel monkeys); and ceboids (capuchins, woolly monkeys, spider monkeys, howler monkeys). This catalog is derived from Sanderson (1957). Most of these groups have not been well studied. Capuchin monkeys, which are at the high end of the New World series, should yield fascinating field observations; they are apparently quite sociable, and captive specimens demonstrate tool-using behavior (Klüver, 1937).

CHAPTER 3

LANGUAGE

IN THE PRECEDING CHAPTER WE ARRANGED the primates in sequence, from tree shrew through man, and considered the order of species without giving unique significance to man. This nonanthropocentric view has a certain appeal, perhaps increasing objectivity in investigating behaviors which have been thought to be uniquely human. Nevertheless, there can be no doubt that human beings differ enormously from chimpanzees, and this chapter focuses on what is probably the major basis of this difference: language. The point to be kept in mind is that just as man differs enormously from chimp, so does chimp differ enormously from baboon. Consider, for example, that chimps are able to recognize themselves in a mirror, but lower primates cannot. Gallup (1970) sees this as evidence that human beings and chimps are the only primates with a self concept. This is a questionable interpretation, but it does emphasize that we are only beginning to look at ways to determine whether the difference between man and chimp is greater or lesser than the difference between chimp and baboon. With this qualification in mind, we will examine language as a possibly unique characteristic of man.

IS LANGUAGE UNIQUELY HUMAN?

Many nonhuman species have characteristic forms of communication. Bees, for example, do not simply buzz. They are known to make at least ten distinctly different sounds, at least some of which appear to have a communication function. When a foraging bee locates a food source, it returns to the hive and communicates the distance and direction of the food through a cyclical "figure eight dance" on the face of the honeycomb. During one portion of the dance cycle the bee moves in a straight run, emitting a series of sound pulses. The time duration of this series is directly proportional to the distance the bee has traveled to the food source. The angle between the straight run and the vertical is equal to the angle between the direction of the food source and the direction of the sun, as in Figure 3–1 (Wenner, 1964; Gould et al., 1970). These communication mechanisms appear to be inherited characteristics of bees.

It is worth considering whether bee communication is language. We usually think of language as being largely learned and, as such, as having a great deal of variability in its use. The stylized inherited signals of bees seem far removed from that idea. If we look at some birds, however, their vocal patterns show learning effects. White-crowned sparrows of different parts of California have songs characteristic of their particular locale. One bird taken from its nest as a fledgling and then exposed to a recorded song from another locale developed a fair copy of the alien song (Marler and Tamura, 1969; Nottebohm, 1970). Assuming that bird songs have some communication function, and it seems likely that they do, the sparrows' regional "dialects" approach our notion of language.

The more we learn about animal communication the harder it becomes to distingish it from language. Several definitions of language have already been offered for that specific purpose, but a definition acceptable to all researchers is yet to be obtained (Lenneberg, 1969; Zajonc, 1969:177; Premack, 1971). One clear way to demonstrate that animals can use language would be to teach them a human language such as English. Just that project has been attempted. Two psychologists, Keith and Cathy Hayes, brought a baby chimp named Viki into their home and raised her like a human baby. Since Viki showed no tendency to pick up English on her own, the Hayeses began using special training techniques and were able to teach her to say close approximations of "mama," "papa," and "cup" by about the age of two. Viki's subsequent use of the word "cup" definitely indicated that it meant "I want a drink" to her (Hayes, 1970). However, in six years Viki learned only four English words and a few additional sounds which were used for specific requests (Gardner and Gardner, 1969).

There have been various interpretations given to the

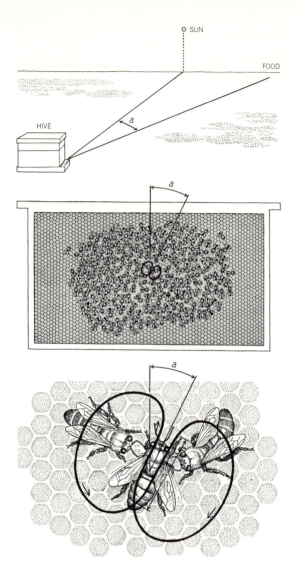

FIGURE 3–1.　Bee dance. Foraging bee must transmit to its hivemates information about the distance from the hive to the food source (*top drawing*) and the angle (*a*) between the direction of the source and the direction of the sun. It does a dance on the honeycomb in which its abdomen describes a kind of figure eight (*middle*). The "straight run" (*A*) of the dance (*bottom*) has a duration proportional to the distance to the food, and it is oriented at an angle from the vertical equal to angle *a*. "Recruit" bees track the dancer's side with their antennae. (From "Sound Communication In Honeybees" by A. Wenner. Copyright © 1964 by Scientific American, Inc. All rights reserved.)

Hayeses' experience, no doubt indicative of the various interpreters' opinions about chimpanzees. At one extreme, the experiment with Viki is interpreted as a demonstration that chimps have no reasonable potential for language. The other side claims that chimps are capable of simple language but not of *spoken* language. That Viki, as an infant, rarely babbled in the manner of human infants (Hayes, 1970) suggests that vocalization is not a convenient motor activity for chimpanzees. Pursuing this line of reasoning, another pair of psychologists, Allen and Beatrice Gardner (1969; 1971) began training a year-old baby chimp named Washoe in a "sign language" of the deaf, whereby various hand movements and configurations are used to represent commonly understood meanings. The method of training was similar to the normal speech training of a human toddler, though more intense. Adults conversed in the sign language in Washoe's presence, and they "spoke" to her and named objects to her. Washoe's first use of many of her signs apparently occurred as a delayed imitation of the human beings. Chimps are very imitative, and some of these behaviors are similar to the imitative behavior of human toddlers. For example, Washoe was bathed regularly as part of her standard routine. One day she filled her little bathtub with water, dunked one of her dolls in the tub, and then dried it with a towel.

A part of the daily routine has been to brush her teeth after every meal. . . . Usually, having finished her meal, Washoe would try to leave her highchair; we would restrain her, signing, "First, toothbrushing, then you can go." One day, during the 10th month of the project, Washoe was visiting the Gardner home and found her way into the bathroom. She climbed up on the counter, looked at our mug full of toothbrushes, and signed "toothbrush." At the time, we believed that Washoe understood the sign but we had not seen her use it. She had no reason to ask for the toothbrushes, because they were all well within her reach, and it is most unlikely that she was asking to have her teeth brushed. This was our first observation, and one of the clearest examples, of behavior in which Washoe seemed to name an object or an event for no obvious motive other than communication. . . . By the 14th month she was making the "toothbrush" sign at the end of meals with little or no prompting; in fact she has called for her toothbrush in a peremptory fashion when its appearance at the end of a meal was delayed. The "toothbrush" sign is not merely a response cued by the end of a meal; Washoe retained her ability to name toothbrushes when they were shown to her at other times.[1] (Gardner and Gardner, 1969:667.)

[1] Copyright 1969 by the American Association for the Advancement of Science. Reprinted with permission of the authors and *Science*.

By the end of the twenty-second month of the project (Washoe was about three years old, which is the maturational equivalent of a four- to five-year-old child), she could make 34 different signs *and use them in appropriate situations,* and her rate of acquisition was accelerating. Her usage showed many similarities to a human toddler's word usage. The sign for "flower" was used for flower pictures as well as for real flowers. She had transferred her "dog" sign to the sound of barking by an unseen dog. The sign for "key" was used to name keys and to ask for them when they were not in sight. (Washoe opens locks.) Her sign for "more" has generalized from a specific reference to tickling (chimps love to be tickled) to other play behavior, to what is apparently a request for repetition of any performance. Originally she was trained to make her "open" sign for three doors she used every day, but it soon generalized to all doors and then to containers such as the refrigerator, drawers, and jars, and she eventually used it to ask that the water faucet be turned on. She spontaneously combines signs, such as "open flower" (to be let through the gate to a flower garden), or "listen eat" (at the sound of an alarm signaling mealtime). At this writing the four-year-old chimp uses meaningful three- and four-word combinations (Gardner and Gardner, 1971).

Another psychologist, David Premack (1970; 1971), has taught a chimp named Sarah to associate colored plastic shapes with words. After two years of training, Sarah's "vocabulary" consists of about 60 nouns, 20 verbs, and 30 additional shapes which represent adjectives, prepositions, and adverbs. Sarah can arrange the shapes on a board in order to make requests. For example, she will line up four shapes to say *Mary give apple Sarah* when she wants one of her trainers (Mary) to give her an apple. The trainer can construct sentences as complex as *Sarah insert banana pail apple dish,* and Sarah will place a banana in a pail and an apple on a dish. She understands modification of this type of sentence (e.g., *Sarah take-out grape dish banana pail* or *Sarah insert apple red dish apple banana green dish*). She understands that one shape represents a question mark and can answer questions of the form: 'Are these two objects the same or different?" (She has shapes for *same* and *different.*)

We do not propose to argue whether or not Washoe and/or Sarah are using language in the sense that human beings do. Certainly their performances are impressive. It would be interesting to see if two chimps trained in the same language would use their signs to communicate with each other. Or, if they were mated, whether their offspring would show any tendency to imitate the parents' signs. These outcomes do not seem particularly unlikely. In fact, it seems reasonable to expect that chimps in the wild may have some simple form of culturally based "sign language." Recent observations of free-ranging chimps suggest that gestural and tactile communications play a major role in interindividual relations (Van Lawick-Goodall, 1968). The key question is whether these communications are innate signs which all chimps understand or whether they have been invented and diffused by a learning process. The fact that a "language" has not yet been discovered may simply be a consequence of our minimal effort at looking for it. Not only chimps but dolphins (Lilly and Miller, 1969) seem to be reasonable language candidates.

We hasten to point out that if our expectations were fulfilled, if behaviorists did come to some consensus that some nonhuman species have language, there would be very little change in our anthropocentric view of the world. There can be little doubt that animal language, if it exists, would be rudimentary in comparison with human language. The fact that human and chimp communication might be "merely" quantitatively different would be irrelevant. Given that our cognitive and cultural behavior is so fully based on language, that quantitative difference would still make us worlds apart.

THE BIOLOGICAL BASIS OF HUMAN LANGUAGE

It would, of course, be possible to take a group of human infants, raise them without using any sort of language, and see if they developed a language on their own and—if so—if there would be similarities between their language and ours. A crude form of that experiment reputedly once was done at the direction of Frederick II. He hypothesized that the children might speak Hebrew or Latin, but they all died before Frederick got his data and to our knowledge the question has never been resolved empirically (Salimbene, cited in Mussen et al., 1963:162).

It seems reasonable to assume that the infants would at least begin the route toward language. Although it is possible to increase an infant's *quantity* of vocalizations through smiling and tickling reinforcement (Rheingold et al., 1969; Weisberg, 1967), it appears that the *capacity* for vocalization develops independently of environmental influences, at least during the first several months of life. All normal human neonates start life with crying sounds, but they soon add vowels as they begin the large group of baby noises collectively known as cooing. At about six months they begin babbling, which is the random repetition of many phonetic elements, apparently for the sheer joy of vocalizing. All babies' babbling sounds are similar regardless of race or culture. It is only as the baby approaches a year that his vocalizations reflect the specific phoneme [2] usage of his culture (Stott, 1967: 255–256).

The spontaneous development of early vocal behavior is best demonstrated by a study which compared babies of congenitally deaf parents with babies of hearing parents during the first three months of life (Lenneberg, 1967:137; 1969). These two groups of infants differed significantly in their exposure to language sounds. An additional difference resulted from the deaf mothers' inability to tell whether their children's facial expressions were accompanied by silence or noise, so that these mothers never responded to their babies' vocalizations per se. The hearing parents' babies vocalized on the occasions of adult vocalizations, whereas the deaf parents' babies did not. Except for that difference, both groups of infants made the same amount of noise and went through the same pattern of vocal development during the three months of the study. Therefore, the infants in our hypothetical experimental group would probably begin to vocalize on their own in spite of their lack of language exposure. There is, of course, considerable doubt that they would agree on the meanings of these vocalizations. However, we would bet that if they did not come to consensus on a spoken language, they would at least develop a system of facial expressions to convey emotional information, and these would be expressions that we all already know. Charles Darwin came to a similar conclusion in his book *The Expression of the Emotions in Man and Animals* (1965), in which he examined the gestures and facial expressions associated with such emotions as grief, love, hatred, anger, guilt, and shame. He concluded that since many of these expressions are identical across races and cultures and among people born blind, and since they also occur in very young children, they must be inherited rather than learned, and communication of emotional feelings by these means must be a characteristic of the human species.

---

[2] Phonemes are the basic sound units of a language.

More recent studies support Darwin's contention that certain gestures are uniform across cultures, and even occasionally between species. Samoan, French, Nilohamitic, and Japanese girls all flirt by first turning toward the man, smiling and raising their eyebrows in a rapid "flash." Then they usually turn away the head or the whole body, with the head often being lowered. In very naive girls, the head is sometimes hidden with one hand (Eibl-Eibesfeldt, 1968:483–484). This explicit averting of one's gaze from another person may be a basic gesture of submissiveness and/or shame and/or embarrassment (Darwin, 1965:320, 345–346). Looking away, or avoiding the gaze of an opponent, is a common sign of submission in nonhuman primates; its converse, the direct gaze or stare, is widely associated with threat and dominance behavior in nonhuman primates (Marler, 1965:571) as well as in human beings. It appears, then, that at least a few gestures have evolved phylogenetically and do not require learning (Andrew, 1963). Thus, the smiling and laughing gestures of children born blind and deaf are essentially normal (Eibl-Eibesfeldt, 1968:483). Therefore, we might expect our specially raised group of infants to use some common gestures to communicate emotional information even though they might have had no opportunity to learn them from adults.

In addition to gestural communication, we might find the apparently universal vocal inflections associated with the giving of commands or making of demands, or with tenderness, anger, fear, excitement, alarm, sexual arousal, play, and humor. As with the gestures, these inflections are mainly concerned with conveying *emotional* information. But human language conveys much information besides the purely emotional, and it is this that suggests the major question: Is there any reasonable chance that a group of infants could develop an ad hoc language appropriate for communicating nonemotional information, and if so, might that language bear any resemblance to common languages? We, of course, do not know.

CAPACITY FOR LANGUAGE

Children from middle-class families generally have greater language skill than children from lower-status families (Stott, 1967:265–267). Lenneberg (1969) has argued that these are socially determined aspects of language usage and are not nearly so important as the individual's underlying biological *capacity* for language. Rather than assessing the development of language by an inventory of vocabulary, by grammatical complexity of sentences, or by clarity of pronunciation, he suggests that we describe a child's language capacity in terms of a few broad developmental milestones, such as those listed in Table 3–1. The chronological ages associated with each milestone are approximate; there is much individual variation. But the particular motor milestones listed in the table do correlate highly with the language mile-

Table 3–1   Developmental milestones in motor and language development *

Approxi-mate age:	Motor development milestones	Language development milestones
3 months	Supports head when in prone position; weight is on elbows; hands mostly open; no grasp reflex.	Markedly less crying than at 8 weeks; when talked to and nodded at, smiles and produces squealing-gurgling sounds usually called *cooing*, which is vowel-like in character and pitch-modulated; sustains cooing for 15–20 seconds.
4 months	Plays with rattle placed in his hands (by shaking it and staring at it), head self-supported.	Responds to human sounds more definitely; turns head; eyes seem to search for speaker; occasionally some chuckling sounds.
6 months	Sits using hands for support; unilateral reaching.	Cooing sounds change to babbling resembling 1-syllable utterances; most common utterances sound somewhat like ma, mu, da, or di.
1 year	Stands; walks when held by one hand.	Signs of understanding some words; applies some sounds regularly to signify persons or objects.

* Adapted from Lenneberg, 1967: 128–130; 1969 with permission of the author and *Science*. Copyright 1969 by the American Association for the Advancement of Science.

1.5 years	Prehension and release fully developed; gait propulsive; creeps downstairs backward.	Repertoire of 3–50 words not joined in phrases; trains of sounds and intonation patterns resembling discourse; good progress in understanding.
2 years	Runs (with falls); walks stairs with one food forward only.	More than 50 words; 2-word phrases most common; more interest in verbal communication; no more babbling.
2.5 years	Jumps with both feet; stands on one foot for one second.	Every day new words; utterances of 3 and more words; seems to understand almost everything said to him; still many grammatical deviations.
3 years	Tiptoes 3 yards; walks stairs with alternating feet; jumps 12 inches.	Vocabulary of some 1,000 words; about 80% intelligibility; grammar of utterances close approximation to colloquial adult language, although mistakes still occur.
4 years	Jumps over rope; hops on one foot; walks on a line.	Language is well established; grammatical anomalies restricted either to unusual constructions or to the more literate aspects of discourse.

stones. Children in diverse cultures display these same correspondences between particular motor and language milestones (Lenneberg, 1967:138). Lenneberg suggests that children from different social classes in the United States do not differ in the development of language *capacity*, as measured by his milestones. We do not know of data testing this hypothesis, but if that is indeed the case, language development may be viewed as one aspect of the general biological development of the child. This is different from the prevailing view of language development as exclusively a learning process. Probably a merger of the two views is in order. One point common to both views is that the organism must reach a certain minimal state of neurological development before it can begin to develop language.

BRAIN DEVELOPMENT
AND LANGUAGE DEVELOPMENT

Several physical parameters of brain development indicate that a major portion of brain maturation occurs in the period between birth and the beginning of language acquisition, at about age two. During the first two years, the brain's weight increases roughly 350 percent over its birth weight, whereas from ages two to twelve there is a weight increase of only 35 percent, and after age twelve there is practically no weight increase at all. Cortical neurons grow considerably in volume (although their number apparently remains constant) during the first two years, and then growth rate decreases until by puberty little change occurs. There are similar rates of change in the decreasing packing density of neurons. Similar rates of change occur in the chemical composition of the brain with the greatest change occurring from birth to about age two, less change thereafter, and practically no change after puberty (Lenneberg, 1967:69, 158–170). We do not yet know of a direct connection between these developments and the acquisition of language, but there is a strong inference that they are related.

During the normal course of language development, language functions usually become localized in the left hemisphere of the brain, probably because the left side is relatively large initially (Geschwind, 1970). Functional lateralization appears to begin at about the age of speech onset and is completed by adulthood. There is apparently a period in early infancy when both brain hemispheres are capable of language functions. Children who receive damage to one hemisphere before the onset of speech still have a good chance for normal onset, irrespective of whether the damage was to the left or the right hemisphere. It appears that when the left hemisphere is damaged at this early age, the right hemisphere is fully able to take over the language functions. After the onset of speech the situation is somewhat changed. Damage to the left hemisphere of an older child is much more likely to result in disturbed speech than damage to the right (Lenneberg, 1967: 142–154).

The extent to which speech functions have become localized in the left hemisphere by adulthood is illustrated in the case of a 49-year-old patient whose hemispheres were surgically separated in a successful effort to control epileptic convulsions. Each hemisphere of the brain is mostly associated with the sensory and motor activities of the *opposite* side of the body. Thus, the right hemisphere controls the left side of the body and the left hemisphere the right side of the body. There is normally a large connecting link between the hemispheres, but that link was severed in the operation. There were no gross changes in the patient's personality or in his above-average intellect. But there were some behavioral oddities apparently caused by cutting communication from the right hemisphere to the language functions in the left hemisphere. The patient could see clearly in both the left and the right halves of his field of vision, and he could read material in the right half, but he could not read material in the left half of his field of vision. Nor could he write anything meaningful with his left hand. He could not carry out verbal commands with his left arm or leg. When an object was presented solely in his left field of vision, or in his left hand, he might react to it appropriately but could not name it or describe it—apparently because this information was in his right hemisphere and therefore isolated from the speech functions in his left hemisphere (Sperry, 1964).

Given the adaptability of very young brains, we might expect that if the hemisphere were separated in a very young child, language functions might develop in both hemispheres. That does seem to have occurred in one boy whose hemispheres had never been connected because of a congenital accident (Sperry, 1964:245). This is consistent with the general finding that full speech recovery after brain damage is more likely to occur the younger the victim, apparently because the younger brain is more adaptable to the injury (Lenneberg, 1967:146–150). Thus, increasing lateralization of speech functions may be related to increasing rigidity of the brain. This suggests that there is a "critical period" for language acquisition which begins at about the age of two, when the brain has reached sufficient maturity for language, and ends sometime before puberty, by which time the brain has lost much of its adaptive ability. Presumably the acquisition of language before or after this critical period would be impossible, or at least very difficult. If such a period does exist, it would conveniently explain why very young children learn two or more languages with ease while adults have great difficulty acquiring a new language and rarely develop the appropriate accent, even after years of total immersion in the "foreign" environment.

CONCLUSIONS

There are major difficulties in deciding if language is a uniquely human characteristic. The essential point is that even if some animals do indeed have language, it is rudimentary relative to human standards. Therefore, since language is so central to our cognitive and cultural processes, it may, for practical purposes, be considered the central differentiator of man from the other species.

The appearance of language in the human child is usually considered the result of the child's learning experiences in his social environment. This is true to a degree. There are, however, indications that *some* aspects of language development consistently occur independently of environmental variation. Human beings may have a biologically based "critical period" for language acquisition, running from about age two to puberty. During this period the brain has reached sufficient physical maturity for the complex task of language learning, and it has not yet lost its adaptive ability to accommodate language functions. Presumably, language acquisition before or after this period is very difficult. Such a critical period could account for the ability of children to learn "foreign" languages much more easily than adults.

Suggested Reading

Charles Darwin's *The Expression of the Emotions in Man and Animals* (University of Chicago Press; Chicago: 1965) is the classic discussion of the biological basis for human communication. A more modern treatment is E. Lenneberg's *Biological Foundations of Language* (Wiley; New York: 1967).

See *Animal Communication,* edited by T. Sebeok (Indiana University Press; Bloomington: 1968) for discussions of social communication in a wide variety of species. S. Altmann's edited collection, *Social Communication Among Primates* (University of Chicago Press; Chicago: 1967) focuses more narrowly on the nonhuman primates.

The Ape in Our House, by C. Hayes (Harper and Brothers; New York: 1951) describes the experiences of a husband and wife team of psychologists who brought a baby chimp into their home in an unsuccessful attempt to teach it spoken language.

PART II

Differences Among Human Beings

We have been looking at behavior as a species characteristic, ignoring differences among individuals or among populations of individuals. The following four chapters will examine some biological factors which differentiate human beings from one another by characteristics relevant to social behavior.

Individuality begins with the information encoded in an embryo's set of genes—its genotype. Some of these genes are shared with each parent and each grandparent, but the particular combination is unique, and that is the basis for the unique physical and behavioral development which is to follow. But if genes characterize the individual, they also characterize the individual's group. The population from which his parents are drawn may be thought of as a breeding population, and the total collection of genes in all the members of that population may be considered a gene pool which is the source of all the genetic information which will be passed on to the next generation. Just as each individual's genotype forms the basis of his subsequent development, the gene pool forms the basis of each breeding population's subsequent development. We begin, then, with genetics—on the individual level in Chapter 4 and on the population level in Chapter 5.

Genotypes are difficult to observe directly, and so in spite of the fact that they are central to an understanding of the biological aspects of behavior, we are severely limited in our studies of behavioral genetics. The neurohormone system is much more open to observation and so forms a particularly appealing area for research in the biology of social behavior. Chapter 6 describes what we are beginning to find out about the role of hormones in mediating social processes. Finally, Chapter 7 will discuss two aspects of biological development in the socialization of the individual.

CHAPTER 4   GENETICS

MENDEL WAS LUCKY WITH HIS PEA PLANTS.
The close fit between his experimental results, discussed below, and theoretical laws of inheritance led statistician R. A. Fisher to suggest that the data had been fudged by one of Mendel's assistants (Fisher, 1965:52). But even if there were methodological inadequacies, there are few today who doubt the value of Mendel's laws in explaining the inheritance of physical characteristics.

In species which reproduce sexually, each new individual receives an equal number of chromosomes from each parent. Each chromosome from the "mother" is homologous to one chromosome from the "father," and the homologous chromosomes come together into pairs in the new individual's cells. A human being receives 23 chromosomes from each parent, for a total of 46. These then form 23 pairs with one chromosome of each pair from each parent.

It is helpful to think of a chromosome as a long string of well-defined gene sites (or *loci*). Within each pair of homologous chromosomes, the loci of one exactly match the loci of the other, so the pair may be thought of as a collection of "locus pairs."

Mendel's laws, stated in modern terms, assume that each locus pair independently determines one inherited characteristic of the individual. Furthermore, there are two types of genes (or *alleles*) which may fit at each site of the locus pair. One allele is *dominant* and the other is *recessive*.

Inherited characteristics are assumed to have two forms; one form is associated with each of the two alleles. If both genes at a locus pair are the same allele, the form of the inherited characteristic will be the form associated with that allele. If the two

41

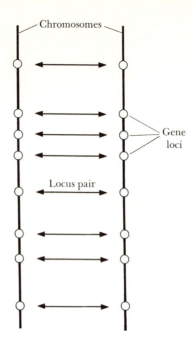

FIGURE 4-1. Schematic view of a pair of homologous chromosomes. One chromosome comes from each parent. The circles along each chromosome represent gene loci. The spacing of loci along one chromosome corresponds exactly to the loci spacing on the other chromosome of the homologous pair. Therefore, each locus on one chromosome has a corresponding locus on the other chromosome. Two corresponding loci are referred to here as a "locus pair." The diagram shows eight locus pairs.

genes are different alleles, the form of the inherited characteristic will be the form associated with the dominant allele. For example, one inherited characteristic of pea plants is the shape of the peas: they may be round or wrinkled. Mendel in effect assumed that one locus pair determined the shape and that the round shape is associated with the dominant allele. Thus, if that locus pair contained two dominant alleles, or one dominant and one recessive, the peas would be round. If the locus pair contained two recessive alleles, the peas would be wrinkled.

Starting with two pure strains of pea plants—one which always gives round peas and one which always gives wrinkled peas—we can predict the results of hybridization. Let R symbolize the round allele and r the wrinkled allele. The pure strain of round peas has only R alleles, and so we can symbolize the two genes occupying its "pea shape" locus pair as RR. The two genes at the same locus pair in the pure wrinkled strain can be symbolized *rr* since there are no *R* alleles in that strain. When the two strains are crossed, each offspring receives one gene for that locus pair from each parent—an *R* from the round-strain parent and an *r* from the wrinkled-strain parent—so that the two genes at the offsprings' "pea shape" locus pair are *Rr*. Since *R* is the dominant allele, all the offspring will have round peas, and they will be visually indistinguishable from their pure round parent. These offspring are called the F_1 generation.

Now we would like to be able to predict what would happen if we crossed two F_1 individuals, but unfortunately we cannot because of the probabilistic nature of Mendel's laws. We can, however, predict the expected outcome of a large number of these crosses. When *Rr* individuals are crossed there is an even chance that any one of their offspring (the F_2 generation) will have received an *R* or *r* from its "father." Similarly, there is an even chance that it will have received an *R* or an *r* from its "mother." Since these probabilities are independent of each other, the combined probability that any one F_2 offspring will be *RR* (i.e., will have received an *R* from each parent) is $(.5)^2 = .25$. Similarly, the probability that any one F_2 offspring will be *rr* is .25.

There are two ways for an F_2 offspring to be *Rr*. It can receive the *R* from its "father" and the *r* from its "mother," or vice versa. In either case, the probability of occurrence is .25, and so taking into account both cases, the total probability of any one F_2 offspring being *Rr* is $2(.25) = .5$. Given these probabilities, we could predict that if there were a large number of F_1 crosses, their F_2 offspring would occur in the proportions: .25 *RR*, .25 *rr*, and .5 *Rr*. The three generations are diagrammed in Figure 4–2. Since *R* is dominant, .75 of the F_2 generation will have round peas (i.e., the *RR* and *Rr* plants), and .25 will have wrinkled peas (i.e., the *rr* plants).

Since it is not possible to visually differentiate between *RR* and *Rr* plants, the genetic composition of the F_1 generation must be confirmed by backcrossing to the pure strains. These two back-crosses are diagrammed in Figure 4–3. Backcross to the dominant pure strain will produce offspring having round peas. Backcross to the recessive pure strain produces a generation where half the plants have round peas and half have wrinkled peas. These easily observable results confirm the genetic composition of the F_1 generation.

Mendel's laws are beautifully simple. Unfortunately, few inherited characteristics actually obey them because there are

Generation

Pure strains:

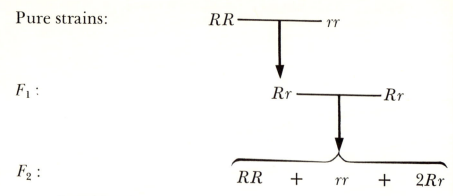

F_1 :

F_2 :

FIGURE 4–2. Inheritance of R and r alleles from two pure strains through to the F_2 generation.

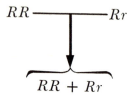

a.   Backcross of F_1 to the dominant pure strain.

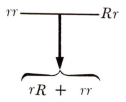

b. Backcross of F_1 to the recessive pure strain.

FIGURE 4–3.   Backcrosses of F_1.

complicating factors: Many inherited characteristics are affected by more than one locus pair; there may be more than two alleles for a given locus pair; locus pairs do not always operate independently of each other. But the most important complication for the present discussion is that very few characteristics are totally inherited; they may be greatly affected by conditions of the environment. Mendel was fortunate that his experiments did not involve any of these complicating factors.

THE INHERITANCE OF BEHAVIOR

Although there has been easy acceptance of the idea that *physical* characteristics can be transmitted genetically, there has been recent scientific resistance to the notion that *behavioral* characteristics may be similarly transmitted. Many psychologists assume that virtually all behavior is learned by the organism through interaction with its physical and social environment—at least among the higher organisms. The human infant is generally considered to have a few inborn reflex actions: sucking, clasping, the pointing reflex which orients the infant's mouth toward the nipple, the Babinski reflex in which the infant spreads its toes when the bottom of its foot is stimulated, and the startle reflex in which the infant throws back its arms when it falls backwards. These reflexes are found in the earliest stage of infancy, and they quickly lose their spontaneous character. Beyond these few "programmed" actions, human behavior and the behavior of most mammals is usually thought to be almost totally learned. In this view, of course, the genetic basis of behavior is insignificant.

Selective breeding experiments have established that behavioral characteristics can be genetically transmitted in mammals. Tyron (1940) gave rats a maze learning task and mated good performers together and poor performers together. A few generations of this artificially selective breeding produced one strain of rats which learned the maze quickly and one strain which learned it slowly. Similar procedures have produced strains of fearful and nonfearful rats (Hall, 1941). Dogs, rats, and chickens have been bred for greater or lesser aggressive behavior. These experiments do not demonstrate that there are "maze-learning genes" or "fear genes," but they do show that the genetic composition of an animal can be manipulated in order to produce fairly consistent effects on behavior, although the mechanisms which connect the animal's genetic makeup to his behavior are largely unknown. It seems likely that these behaviors are partly mediated by variations in physical (especially nerve) structure, hormonal balance, and sensory processes.

Scott and Fuller (1965) carried out a long series of dog breeding experiments to study genetic effects on canine social behavior. They raised puppies of five pure breeds under standard conditions of feeding, training, and environment. By holding these environmental factors constant, they were able to verify the popular laymen's notion that breeds differ in behavior and temperament for biological reasons. For example, basenjis and wire-haired terriers are generally more aggressive than cocker spaniels, although there is extreme variation within the breeds as well as between them. The basenjis and spaniels differed on the largest number of behavioral traits measured, and so they were selected for an elaborate cross-breeding experiment to determine if the inheritance of behavior characteristics followed the simple Mendelian laws.

The puppies were left almost undisturbed until the age of five weeks when they were put into contact with a human handler. At that time the basenji pups characteristically showed much higher avoidance of the handler than the spaniels did, although by the age of seven weeks the basenjis were almost as tame as the spaniels. All puppies were scored at five weeks on their degree of avoidance and fearful vocalization in response to the human handler. Using an arbitrary criterion level which separated "low avoidance" scores from "high avoidance" scores, .85 of the spaniel pups, but only .26 of the basenjis showed low avoidance of the handler.

When basenjis and spaniels were crossed, .25 of the F_1 generation showed low avoidance. That is, the F_1 generation behaved statistically in a manner almost identical to that of their basenji parents. This is exactly what would be expected if the characteristic "low avoidance" were associated with a single locus pair and if the basenji allele for that pair were dominant and the spaniel allele were recessive. Assuming for the moment that this is the case, we can calculate the proportion of low avoiders in the F_2 generation—i.e., the offspring of the F_1 generation. As demonstrated above, .25 of any F_2 generation will have two dominant alleles, .5 will have one dominant and one recessive allele, and .25 will have two recessive alleles. Therefore .75 of the F_2 dogs should be basenji in avoidance behavior, and .25 should be spaniel in avoidance behavior. Since pure basenjis have a .26 probability of low avoidance, and spaniels have a .85 probability, the expected proportion of low avoiders in the F_2 generation is $(.75)(.26) + (.25)(.85) = .41$. In fact, .39 of that generation were low avoiders, and so the calcuation fits the observed data quite well.

Still using the simple Mendelian assumptions, we can calculate the percentage of low avoiders if the F_1 dogs are backcrossed to the original pure strains. As explained above, if F_1 dogs are backcrossed to the pure dominant strain (i.e., the basenjis) all offspring will have at least one dominant allele, so that these pups should behave similarly to the pure basenji—i.e., .26 should be low avoiders. In fact, .17 of the pups from this backcross were actually low avoiders, so the calculation is clearly not perfect, but still not too far off.

If F_1 dogs are backcrossed to the pure recessive strain (i.e., the spaniels), then half of the resulting offspring will have one dominant and one recessive allele—these should behave like basenjis—and half will have two recessive alleles—these should behave like spaniels. The expected proportion of low avoiders is (.5) (.26) + (.5) (.85) = .56. In fact, .47 of these offspring were low avoiders; again, the prediction is not perfect but close.

Figure 4–4 summarizes the results of these various crosses. The generally close agreement between the observed proportions

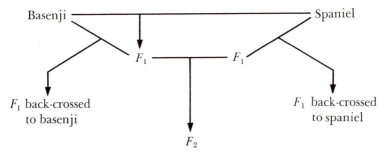

a. A schematic diagram of the various basenji- spaniel crosses.

FIGURE 4–4. Basenji-Cocker crosses.

	Theoretical proportion	Observed proportion	n
Pure basenji	–	.26	27
Pure spaniel	–	.85	26
F_1 cross between basenji and spaniel	.26	.25	52
F_2 generation	.41	.39	74
F_1 backcrossed to basenji	.26	.17	42
F_1 backcrossed to spaniel	.56	.47	30

b. Theoretical and observed proportions of "low avoiders" in the various basenji-spaniel crosses. (Adapted from Scott and Fuller, 1965: 267) .

of low avoiders and the theoretically calculated proportions is good evidence that avoidance behavior in dogs is associated with one locus pair and in that sense is genetically similar to Mendel's pea plant characteristics. Most of the other behavior characteristics which were observed, however, do not follow the simple Mendelian rules so well; they require two or more locus pairs, as well as some additional assumptions, to satisfactorily explain the data. In general we cannot expect behavioral characteristics to be associated with single locus pairs. But there can be little doubt that genes contribute significantly to the variation in many behaviors within species as high as dogs. Of course, what is true for dogs may not be true for man. Comparable experiments on human beings obviously cannot be done. The most direct evidence for the genetic basis of human behavior comes from the study of intelligence in twins.

There are two types of twins: *monozygotic* and *dizygotic*. Monozygotic twins occur when about one in every 300 fertilized eggs subsequently divides in two resulting in two individuals who are genetically identical. Dizygotic twins occur when two separate eggs are fertilized at the same time. These twins share the same uterine environment, but they are no closer genetically than any other pair of sibs, which means that on the average they share 50 percent of their genes.[1] Monozygotic twins are always of the same sex while dizygotics are equally likely to be of the same or of different sexes. There are about two pairs of dizygotic twins in a given population for every pair of monozygotic twins.

Twin studies usually compare monozygotic and dizygotic twins on the assumption that twin partners will grow up in similar environments, and therefore any differences which appear between dizygotic twins, but not monozygotic twins, will be due to hereditary differences. For example, Figure 4–5 presents correlations of IQ test performances for monozygotic twins raised together, monozygotic twins raised separately, and dizygotic twins raised together. Comparison of the first and second rows shows that differences in test performance can occur in spite of identical heredity if the environments are different. Comparing the first and third rows, we see that, under the assumption of similar environments for twins raised together, IQ is largely dependent on heredity. Some caution must be used in interpreting these

[1] We are following a common but sloppy usage. Presumably, all human beings hold some genes in common. When we say that two people "share 50 percent of their genes," we really mean 50 percent of that subset of genes which may vary from one person to another.

Figure 4–5.   Correlation of intelligence in twins (Lenz, 1963:171).

	Binet	Otis	Stanford educational
		IQ test	
Monozygotic twins, raised together (*n* = 50 pairs)	.91	.92	.96
Monozygotic twins, raised separately (*n* = 19 pairs)	.67	.73	.62
Dizygotic twins, raised together (*n* = 50 pairs)	.64	.62	.88

results, however, because it is not clear that dizygotic twins raised together have as similar environments as monozygotic twins raised together.

Oftentimes nutrition and other factors in the intrauterine environment may be systematically different for the two groupings. While all of the monozygotic twin pairs are same-sexed, it must be that only about half of the dizygotic pairs are same-sexed. Since we know that boys are generally treated differently from girls, we must assume that the different-sexed pairs of dizygotic twins are not really experiencing as similar environments as the same-sexed pairs. Presumably, then, the lower correlation betwen dizygotic twins is partly due to genetic differences and partly due to the different sex of some dizygotic twin pairs. This very common difficulty may be avoided if dizygotic twins are divided into same-sexed and different-sexed pairs, as in Figure 4–6. When this is done there is indeed a difference in IQ correlation in the expected direction: same-sexed dizygotic twins have a higher correlation than different-sexed twins. We still find the IQ correlation for monozygotic twins to be substantially higher,

Figure 4–6.   Median values of the correlations of intelligence in twins, taken from nearly all such correlations reported in the literature (adapted from Jensen, 1969:49).

	Median value of correlation	Number of studies
Monozygotic twins, raised together	.87	14
Monozygotic twins, raised separately	.75	4
Dizygotic twins, same sex, raised together	.56	11
Dizygotic twins, different sex, raised together	.49	9

however, and so our initial reckless conclusion that IQ is largely dependent on heredity is still valid under these more cautious conditions.

There are some caveats here. Dizygotic twins are less similar in appearance than monozygotics, and this may decrease the similarity of environmental experiences for the dizygotic twin pair. There is also the problem of large errors in psychological measurement. For genetically identical twins raised together, this measurement error can only increase the differences. For dizygotic twins who are different to begin with, this error can increase or decrease a difference, so that these measurement errors are not really comparable for monozygotic and dizygotic twins (F. Lenz, in W. Lenz, 1963:172). We should also note that in most cases of twins being raised apart, they are still raised in families of similar subculture and socioeconomic level, and so this environmental variance usually is not as great as it might be.

MODIFICATION OF INNATE BEHAVIOR

An enormous amount of argument and misunderstanding would be avoided if we could bury the notion that innate behavior is immutable, totally determinate, and "wired-in" in unvarying step-by-step detail. It is easy to see how the idea of "preprogrammed instincts" must have appealed to early biologists who observed that all members of some particular species showed almost exactly the same complex behavior patterns in all their detail. Consider, for example, lovebirds.

Eight of the nine species of lovebirds make their nests in pre-existing tree cavities which they enter through a small entranceway. The females of all species prepare their nesting materials by punching a series of closely spaced holes in a pliable material such as paper, bark, or a leaf. "The material is held between the upper and lower portions of the bill, which then works like a train conductor's ticket punch" (Dilger, 1962:96). The strips cut out in this manner are then transported to the nest site and used for construction. The actual building and design of the nest are characteristics of the particular species. The Madagascar lovebird simply drops strips of leaf and bark to the bottom of its tree cavity. The peach-faced lovebird works its strips into a well-shaped nest within the cavity. A third species, Fischer's lovebird, constructs an elaborate covered nest with a tunnel entrance inside the tree.

There are striking species differences in the manner of transporting building materials to the nest site. Fischer's lovebird carries the material in its bill, like most birds. The peach-faced lovebird, however, erects its entire plumage, tucking six to eight strips of bark and leaf into the feathers, and then flies off. Some pieces fall out, but the bird usually arrives at its nest site with about half the original cargo still in its feathers.

Since baby lovebirds hatch out after the nests have been constructed, and considering that nest building takes place in the privacy of a tree cavity, it is hard to believe that these highly regularized species-specific forms of nest building and material transportation are learned. It is tempting to think of the whole step-by-step operation as being "instinctively" programmed into the individuals of each species. If that were indeed the case—if these operations are immutably determined by each species' genetic heritage—we would expect a cross breed of two species to produce F_1 offspring which also show immutable nesting operations. Given all the possible complicating factors which distort simple Mendelian prediction, we will not endeavor to specify exactly what the form of F_1 nesting behaviors would be, but it is clear that whatever form they do take should be immutable if the "instinct" assumption is correct. Fischer's and peach-faced lovebirds hybridize easily, and William Dilger (1962) has observed the nesting behavior of the F_1 hybrids. It is not at all immutable.

When our hybrids first began to build their nests, they acted as though they were completely confused. They had no difficulty in cutting strips, but they could not seem to determine whether to carry them in the feathers or in the bill. They got material to the nest sites only when they carried it in the bill, and in their first effort at nest building they did carry in their bills 6 per cent of the time. After they had cut each strip, however, they engaged in behavior associated with tucking. Even when they finally carried the material in the bill, they erected the feathers of the lower back and rump and attempted to tuck. But if they were able to press the strips into their plumage—and they were not always successful in the attempt—they could not carry it to the nest site in that fashion. Every strip dropped out.

Two months later, after they had become more experienced, the hybrids carried many more of their nest strips in their bills—41 per cent, to be exact. But they continued to make the movements associated with the intention to tuck: they erected their rump plumage and turned their heads to the rear, flying away with the materials in their bills only after attempting to tuck.

After two more months had passed they began to learn that strips could be picked up in the bill and carried off with a minimum of prior abortive tucking. But it took two years for them to learn to diminish actual tucking activity to any great extent, and even then they continued to perform many of the movements associated with tucking.

(Three years later) . . . the hybrids are behaving, by and large, like Fischer's lovebird. . . . Only infrequently do they attempt to tuck strips into their plumage (Dilger, 1962:96–97).[2]

These hybrids apparently have a strong innate predisposition toward tucking, but it is clear that the behavior pattern is not immutable. To the contrary, in spite of the apparent reluctance of the bird, it is highly modifiable. It seems likely that there are very few, if any, species in which behavior patterns are totally fixed. Even one-celled animals have been shown to modify their behavior as a result of experience (Corning and Von Burg, 1970).

Many early discussants of innate behavior apparently failed to recognize its intrinsic modifiability, and were distracted by such questions as: "How can an individual's behavior be *genetically determined* if that behavior shows variation over time?" This is not a meaningful question because probably no behavior is "genetically determined." Genes themselves do not do the behaving; the individual who develops from the genes does the behaving. Genes can predispose the developing organism toward one set of behaviors rather than another, but the actual developed form of behavior will depend on the experience of development. Even physical characteristics such as size and structure are not totally determined by the inheritance of genes. For example, the American-born offspring of Mexican and European migrants grow up to be taller than their parents, apparently because of increased quantities or better nutritional quality of food in American diets (Lasker, 1969:1482–1483). And although an individual's IQ is genetically based, *shifts* in his IQ during childhood appear to be unrelated to genetic factors (McCall, 1970).

Of course, the fact that innate behavior is modifiable does not imply that it can be shaped any way at all; the individual's genes do set some limitations. Mongolism, for example, is associated with an abnormal extra chromosome, and the behavior of some mongoloids can be modified by suitable training, but it appears that no amount of training could bring the mongoloid's intelligence level up to the average of the general population.[3]

CAUSATION AND CORRELATION

The only immutable thing that passes from generation to generation is the gene. (And even genes occasionally mutate.) The particular collection of genes in any one individual is unique except in the special case of identical twins. An individual's collection of genes—his inheritance—is called his *genotype*. The genotype is not directly observable. It is possible to look at individual chromosomes, and a single gene has recently been photographed for the first time, but in general it is not yet technically feasible to directly identify separate genes. Therefore, the composition of the genotype must be inferred from the individual's physical and behavioral characteristics, which are observable. These observables are the result of the interaction of the genetic information with the environment and are collectively called the individual's *phenotype*.

Using these terms, the question of genetic causation becomes: Is the occurrence of some feature of the genotype sufficient to insure the occurrence of some characteristic of the phenotype? In mongolism, the presence of an extra "number 21" chromosome is sufficient (but not necessary) to insure that one characteristic of the phenotype is feeble-mindedness, and in that sense one might say that particular feature of the genotype *causes* feeble-mindedness. Unfortunately, we cannot expect all cases of genetic causation to be so clear cut. Assume for a moment that the limits which mongolism places on intelligence were not so severe. That is, assume that with sufficient specialized training or chemical treatment a mongoloid's intelligence level could be raised to the average level of the population. If that were the case,

[3] Mongolism, or Down's syndrome, is characterized by gross mental retardation, growth retardation, abnormal handprints, folds on the eyelids, and susceptibility to leukemia.

A mother over 45 is about eighty times more likely to give birth to a mongoloid than a mother under 30, which suggests that the abnormality may stem from a defect of older eggs. There is some indication of temporal and geographic trends in mongoloid birth rates, which suggests that some sort of environmental factor—perhaps a virus—is also involved. It is not known whether this genetic problem is transmitted from one generation to another (Lerner, 1968:196–197: Lilienfeld, 1969).

the extra chromosome would not be a sufficient condition to insure feeble-mindedness. It would give the individual a particularly high probability of being feeble-minded, but would not necessarily cause feeble-mindedness. We expect this sort of situation to become common in the study of behavioral genetics, and we fear that discussions of causality will be bogged down in ambiguity. In order to avoid these difficulties we will not directly address the question of causality. We will confine ourselves to consideration of whether a particular phenotype is correlated with a particular genotype, and, if so, whether the correlation is spurious or not.[4] (A nonspurious correlation is a necessary condition for causality but not a sufficient condition.) It is this approach which we will use in our following discussions of different behaviors associated with the male and female genotypes.

BEHAVIORAL CORRELATES OF SEX GENOTYPE

All human cells have 46 chromosomes except for the male sperm and the female egg, each of which have only 23 chromosomes. When the sperm and egg combine, the resulting *zygote*— the first cell of the new individual—has 46 chromosomes, half from each parent. Two of these 46 chromosomes are the sex chromosomes; one comes from each parent. The mother always contributes an X-type sex chromosome, while the father may contribute either an X- or Y-type sex chromosome. If the new individual's two sex chromosomes are XX, it is a girl; if the two are XY, it is a boy. It is the father's contribution which determines the sex of the child.

Each sex chromosome has a very large number of genes. Some of these genes determine (apparently through hormonal mechanisms) primary sexual characteristics, such as the presence of testes and ovaries, and secondary sexual characteristics, such as facial hair and breast development. Presumably, the numerous genes in the sex chromosomes are not limited to these physical characteristics. Some *may* be associated with such behavioral characteristics as gender role, aggressiveness or passivity.

The term "gender role" refers to "those things a person says or does to disclose himself or herself as having the status of boy

---

[4] Two variables, *x* and *y*, may be directly related, or they may be indirectly related through some third variable, *z*. In either case, measurements of *x* will correlate with measurements of *y*, but in the second case we say the correlation is "spurious."

or girl, man or woman" (Hampson, 1965:113). The gender role includes sex-appropriate daydreams and fantasies of romantic courtship, marriage, and sometimes of heterosexual erotic play. It essentially refers to the tendency to think of oneself as either a male or a female. Many writers have assumed that these sex-appropriate psychological attitudes are biologically determined by an innate sex drive. There is certainly no question that gender role is highly correlated with sexual genotype. Our concern here is to question whether or not that correlation is spurious. It is conceptually simple to design an experiment to test this: Raise some girl infants as boys and some boy infants as girls, and see whether their eventual gender role corresponds to the sex of their genotype or the sex of their childrearing. Nature has unfortunately provided the experiment for us in the situation of certain hermaphrodites i.e., human beings who are assigned at birth to a sex which is inconsistent with their genotype and raised accordingly.

Let us review here the variables of sex before proceeding further. There are 1) the sex of the genotype (XX or XY); 2) gonadal sex (ovaries or testes); 3) hormonal sex which is correlated to secondary sexual characteristics; 4) the appearance of external genitalia; 5) internal reproductive structures; 6) sex assignment at birth and subsequent rearing; and 7) gender role. Most individuals are consistent on all seven of these variables, but some are not, and these inconsistent individuals are defined as hermaphroditic (Hampson, 1965:109). Of particular concern here are those hermaphrodites who have been assigned a sex at birth which is inconsistent with their genotype. This may occur, for example, in the case of an XY male who is born with an underdeveloped penis, mistakenly classified as a girl, and then raised according to that classification.

Hampson (1965) reports studies on 19 hermaphroditic patients who had been assigned to and reared in a sex which was inconsistent with their genotype. (Five were XX and 14 were XY.) Without exception, the gender role corresponded to the sex of assignment and rearing rather than to the chromosomal sex. It appears that the genotype is mainly relevant in determining the sex of assignment, and that subsequent childrearing then socializes the individual into his appropriate gender role. The high correlation between gender role and genotype is spurious.

The socialization effect appears to be extremely strong. Of 25 hermaphroditic patients who had a contradiction between their external genital appearance and their sex of assignment and rearing (21 had predominantly male genital appearance and 4 had predominantly female appearance), 23 had come to terms with his or her contradictory appearance and had established a gender role totally consistent with the sex of assignment and rearing. The two individuals who did not make this consistent adjustment had predominantly female genital appearance. Both had experienced reassignment of sex from female to male, one by medical advice and the other at his own initiative. Not surprisingly, both had profound psychological problems over their ambivalent gender roles.

THE SEXUAL BASIS OF AGGRESSION

In general, males are more aggressive than females. This does not mean that any given male will be more aggressive than any given female; that is certainly not true. But on the average, men are more aggressive than women (Maccoby, 1966:323–326). "Among adults, men commit more homicides, more suicides, and are arrested more frequently for assault and battery. In adolescence, male delinquency is far more frequently aggressive than is female delinquency. These sex differences extend downward in the age scale at least to the age of three years" (Sears, 1965:136–137). The difference is fairly general across cultures. Boys are found to engage in physical aggression more than girls in such diverse societies as India, Okinawa, the Philippines, Mexico, Kenya, and New England (J. Whiting, Child, Lambert, and B. Whiting, as reported in Beach, 1965:129). This cross-cultural consistency suggests that aggressiveness is a genetically based social behavior which is linked to the male sex chromosome in humans.

An individual's level of aggressiveness may be effected by many genes, some occurring on the 44 nonsexual chromosomes. But the strong correlation between sex and aggressiveness suggests that some of this presumed genetic material would appear on the Y (male) sex chromosome. Unfortunately, we have no way of looking directly for an "aggression gene." We must be content with asking whether the correlation between sex genotype and aggression is spurious. The most common explanations which would make the genotype-phenotype correlation spurious are those based on some sort of social learning (Mischel, 1966; Kohlberg, 1966). Such explanations assume that the culture defines males as more aggressive, and so the male is socialized to be relatively aggressive. This is similar to the explanation of gender roles, and it is probably true, but we question whether it is the whole truth.

Harlow has done extensive studies on rhesus monkeys raised from infancy without real mothers but with cloth dummies serving as surrogate mothers. When these monkeys are put together into daily play groups, males show more aggressive threat behavior than females. These differences are significant as early as two-and-a-half months and increase with age. "It is extremely difficult for us to believe that these differences are cultural, for we cannot imagine how our inanimate surrogate mothers could transmit culture to their infants" (Harlow, 1965:240).

Furthermore, if pregnant rhesus are given the male hormone androgen, their female infant offspring show aggressive behaviors (rough-and-tumble play, facial threats) which greatly exceed those shown by normal females but are more typical of infant males (Young, Goy, and Phoenix, 1964; Goy, 1970). Of course, the fact of a biological basis for aggression in monkeys does not guarantee that a similar mechanism operates in man, but it must be taken as evidence in that direction.

The data available from human beings are more equivocal; however, the fact that the sex difference exists in diverse cultures does seem to be most easily explainable by a genetic hypothesis. D'Andrade, in commenting on the six-culture study by Whiting et al., referred to above, notes:

Although the differences recorded above may be due to differential child-training practices rather than to innate sex-linked behavioral tendencies, the fact that the largest sex differences occur in the younger (three to six) rather than in the older (seven to ten) group gives less weight to the training hypothesis, which would predict the opposite result (D'Andrade, 1966:191).

It appears that male aggressiveness may be effected by both sex-linked genes and the cultural definition of "male." Social learning would reinforce and shape the biological tendency. In fact, the biological tendency could explain why so many cultures include aggressiveness in their male definition. If males were "naturally" more aggressive, the society would come to expect them to be more aggressive and would define them as such.

Popular attempts to explain aggression solely on the basis of a biological instinct seem naive. An individual's aggressive behavior is clearly effected by many nongenetic factors. Child-rearing practices (Sears et al., 1958), frustrating situations (Dollard et al., 1939; Berkowitz, 1969), observation of the aggressive behavior of another person (Bandura and Walters, 1963), the presence of impersonal aggressive stimuli in the external environment (Berkowitz, 1968), obedience to authority (Milgram, 1963), and external constraints all influence the occurrence of aggression. Furthermore, the *forms* in which aggression is displayed must largely be learned. With all these qualifications in mind, we cautiously assert that the correlation between sex genotype and aggression is nonspurious.

THE *XYY* ABNORMALITY AND AGGRESSIVENESS

A normal person has two sex chromosomes: XY if male, XX if female. There are, however, abnormal individuals who have more than two, or only one (Mittwoch, 1967). Thus, some males have one or more "extra" Y chromosomes. Now, if the presence of one Y chromosome in normal males is associated with high aggressiveness (relative to normal females who have no Y chromosomes), it seems reasonable to hypothesize that an abnormal male with two Y's might be unusually aggressive. Recent reports that such XYY males are found in surprisingly high number in maximum security mental institutions appear to support this hypothesis, and the notion that an XYY genotype increases the probability of criminal aggressiveness has received much popular attention (Montagu, 1968a).

The XYY syndrome is an active area of research, but most of the results to date are equivocal, and so our analysis must be regarded as tentative. We will proceed as before and consider two separate questions: (1) Is the presence of the XYY abnormality correlated with aggressiveness? and, if so, (2) Is the correlation spurious?

In examining the correlation data we must introduce a qualification. Most of the studies have been done on inmate populations in maximum security institutions for the mentally ill.[5] The fact that an individual is an inmate does not guarantee that he is highly aggressive, although the inmate population taken as a whole is presumably highly aggressive relative to the general male population.

---

[5] Therefore, the only forms of aggression under study are those which are socially disapproved. We are not aware of any genetic studies on populations characterized by socially valued aggressiveness, examples of which are rising young business executives or war heroes.

Much of the *XYY* research is difficult to evaluate because of inappropriate control groups. For example, some studies show that *XYY* inmates are no more aggressive than chromosomally normal inmates (Kessler and Moos, 1970). All this shows is that the *XYY*'s are not the *most* aggressive inmates. The relevant question is not whether *XYY*'s are more aggressive than other highly aggressive people, but whether they are more aggressive than average. Another problem is that most investigators have confined their sampling to tall inmates because *XYY* individuals tend to be tall. We do not know what proportion of noninstitutionalized tall men have *XYY* abnormalities, and so this work is not helpful in assessing the correlation between the genotype and aggressiveness.

The few general chromosomal surveys of inmate populations show *XYY*'s to constitute from 1.0 percent to 2.9 percent of the males. Chromosome surveys of newborn populations have shown *XYY*'s to constitute from .1 percent to .4 percent of the male births. The *XYY*'s do appear to constitute a better than chance proportion of the presumably aggressive inmate populations (Kessler and Moos, 1970; Razavi, 1969; Lubs and Ruddle, 1970). But, a relatively large number of other sex chromosome abnormalities have also turned up in these populations. For example, the *XXY* genotype has been found to constitute from 1.0 percent (Bartlett et al., 1968; Razavi, 1969) to 1.3 percent (Casey et al., 1966) of similar inmate populations, while its incidence among newborn males is believed to be between .1 percent and .2 percent (Kessler and Moos, 1970; Lubs and Ruddle, 1970; Van den Berghe, 1970). The *XXY* are, then, also disproportionately represented among the institutionalized subjects, and that cannot be taken as evidence for the hypothesis that an extra *Y* leads to extra aggressiveness. It appears that sexual abnormalities of all sorts may be disproportionately represented in the subject populations and that there may not be anything special about the *XYY* abnormality per se.

If we accept the existence of a correlation between the *XYY* genotype and aggressiveness, or more generally between any male sex chromosomal abnormality and aggressiveness, we must then inquire whether or not that correlation is spurious. Many factors have been suggested which would render the relationship spurious. *XYY* people tend to be tall, and this could encourage aggressive activities; or, as Hunter has suggested, their height might make them look dangerous and so bias the court and psychiatrists toward having them institutionalized for community safety (Kessler and Moos, 1970). However, one study of four groups of nonpsychotic, nonretarded juvenile offenders in institutions found that their average height did not differ significantly from population means established for the same age and race groupings (Hook and Kim, 1971).

Abnormalities in the sexual genotype are occasionally associated with morphological abnormalities such as undescended testes, unusually appearing genitalia, or inappropriate secondary sexual characteristics (Kessler and Moos, 1970; Hampson, 1965). These physical oddities might encourage the development of an antisocial individual. Chromosome abnormalities may be associated with mental retardation (Mittwoch, 1967:109; Polani, 1969), and this could certainly explain the relatively high proportion of chromosomally abnormal inmates. It has been suggested that sex chromosome abnormalities may be most frequent at the lower socioeconomic levels, and since it appears that inmate populations are largely drawn from the lower classes, this could render the correlation spurious (Kessler and Moos, 1970).

In sum, although there is little evidence linking the XYY genotype directly to aggressiveness, there does appear to be a disproportionately large number of XYY individuals in maximum security mental institutions. But there is equally good evidence that XXY and possibly other sex chromosomal abnormalities are also overrepresented in these institutions. Many additional variables have been suggested which would render the correlations between genotype and institutionalization spurious. This is an active area of research, and it is hoped that firmer conclusions will be available shortly.[6]

[6] There are some interesting indications that the effects of the sex chromosomes are not necessarily due to genes situated along their length. The Y chromosome is much shorter than the X chromosome, and so the model presented earlier in the chapter of two homologous chromosomes with matching gene positions is not really appropriate for the XY pair, although it is possible that a portion of the X is homologous with the Y (Mittwoch, 1967). Perhaps the *quantity* of sex chromosomal material is relevant for the determination of sex characteristics. The best example of this comes from the study of fingerprints. Women have fewer finger ridges than men. The hypothesis that this is due to the larger quantity of sex chromosome material in women, rather than to differences in the genes per se, may be tested by using the fingerprints of genetically abnormal individuals. Thus, the following series of normal and abnormal sexual genotypes increases in quantity of sex chromosome material: XO, XY (normal male), XX (normal female), XYY, XXY, $XXYY$, XXXX. The average number of finger ridges of individuals with these different genotypes decreases along the series (Polani, 1969; Razavi, 1969). Therefore, in the case of fingerprints at least, there is a strong suggestion that the quantity of sex chromosomes explains sexual variation.

SCHIZOPHRENIA

There is a long history of dispute among psychiatric theorists as to whether schizophrenia is genetically transmitted or if it is mainly the result of faulty family relationships. The theoretical problems are compounded by ambiguities in the diagnosis and definition of schizophrenia. Most clinicians seem to agree that schizophrenia includes two types of symptoms: those associated with *cognition,* and those associated with *social withdrawal.*

The cognitive symptoms are disturbances of language and thought, distortions of the body image, retreat from reality to fantasy, hallucinations, and delusions. The social withdrawal symptoms are fear of others, avoidance of relationships with others, and isolation from others (Buss and Buss, 1969:2).

There is an accumulation of schizophrenia studies which are consistent with a genetic hypothesis. A monozygotic (genetically identical) twin of a schizophrenic person is about four times more likely to be schizophrenic than a dizygotic (genetically dissimilar) twin. Among all classes of relatives, the closer the genetic relationship to a schizophrenic person the higher the likelihood of schizophrenia in the relative (Heston, 1970). But, the genetic hypothesis is not the only one which fits these results. An equally good case may be made for a theory of socially induced schizophrenic disease. Closer relatives have more similar social environments, and it is this sharing of social environments that accounts for the high coincidence of schizophrenia among close relatives.

More recent studies have effectively excluded this social explanation by using subjects raised in adoptive or foster homes. In one study (Heston, 1970), the 47 experimental subjects were adults who had been born to schizophrenic mothers but who were removed from them during the first month of life. These were compared with a control group of 50 adults who had also been separated from their mothers in the first month of life, but these mothers had no record of psychiatric disturbance. Eleven percent of the experimental subjects, but none of the control subjects, developed schizophrenia, which well demonstrates the genetic hypothesis.

The experimental group also showed an excess of various nonschizophrenic disorders. They were more likely to have antisocial personalities (19 percent versus 4 percent), neurotic personality disorders (28 percent versus 14 percent), to have spent more than a year in a penal or psychiatric institution (23 percent versus 4 percent), and they had lower IQ's (94.0 versus 103.7). These are indicators of "schizoid" behavior, which is similar to schizophrenia but does not show well-marked thought disorder, delusions, and hallucinations (Heston, 1970:251). Apparently, not only schizophrenia but also these lesser schizoid behaviors is genetically based. Perhaps the social environment determines whether a "genetically primed" individual will be schizophrenic, or simply schizoid, or normal.

SOCIAL INTROVERSION-EXTRAVERSION

Social introversion-extraversion may be broadly defined to include "sociability, social anxiety, friendliness to strangers, and social spontaneity. So conceived, the behavior dimension may be thought to extend from shy, introspective, anxious withdrawal to friendly, extraverted, self-confident engagement with the interpersonal environment" (Scarr, 1969:824). Scarr's own twin study, plus nine earlier twin studies which she reviewed, shows monozygotic twin pairs to be more similar on measures of social introversion-extraversion than dizygotic twin pairs, thus indicating a genotype-phenotype correlation for introversion-extraversion. There is, of course, the possibility that this correlation is the spurious result of identical twins' having more similar social environments than dizygotic twins. However, in another twin study, Shields compared monozygotic twins who had been raised together with monozygotic twins who had been raised apart since early childhood. The extraversion ratings of those raised together showed an intrapair correlation of .42; those raised apart correlated .61 (Shields, 1962:69). Since the twins raised apart had a higher correlation than those raised together, the relation between genotype and social introversion-extraversion does not appear to be a spurious effect of similar environments.

CONCLUSIONS

Substantial evidence indicates that an individual's behavior is influenced by his genotype. This does not mean that the genes immutably predetermine behavioral characteristics. To the contrary, genetically based behaviors appear to be greatly modifiable through interaction with the physical and social environment.

We have taken a limited approach to the relationships between specific genotypes and behaviors, asking only whether they are correlated, and, if so, whether the correlation is spurious. Of course, any conclusion that such a correlation is nonspurious is necessarily tentative since there is always the possibility that some variable which has escaped our attention would render the relationship spurious. Nonetheless, this approach is convenient because it avoids some of the messy problems associated with the notion of genetic causation.

On the basis of available evidence, we have tentatively concluded that the sexual genotypes are nonspuriously correlated to aggressiveness but not to gender role. The *XYY* genotype, as well as other abnormalities of the male genotype, are correlated to criminal or antisocial aggressiveness (as measured by confinement in a maximum security mental institution), but this may be spurious. Schizophrenic and schizoid behaviors are nonspuriously correlated to some as yet unspecified genotype. Social introversion-extraversion also appears to be nonspuriously correlated to an unspecified genotype.

Suggested Reading

I. M. Lerner has written a good clear introductory genetics text entitled *Heredity, Evolution and Society* (W. H. Freeman; San Francisco: 1968) on the implications of genetic mechanisms for human societies.

Genetics and the Social Behavior of the Dog, by J. Scott and J. Fuller (University of Chicago Press; Chicago: 1965) is a comprehensive account of the authors' elaborate experimentation on the genetic basis of social behavior in several breeds of dogs.

Two collections of papers which provide a great deal of advanced material relevant to behavioral genetics are *Methods and Goals in Human Behavior Genetics*, edited by S. Vandenberg (Academic Press; New York: 1965); and *Sex and Behavior*, edited by F. Beach (Wiley; New York: 1965).

CHAPTER 5   POPULATION
               GENETICS

THE HUMAN POPULATION OF THE WORLD
may be divided into a number of *breeding populations,* each
having an associated *gene pool.* These breeding populations are
so defined that a man in one is more likely to breed with a woman
from the same population than from any other breeding population. The boundaries of these populations are not sharp; there
is usually some degree of interbreeding among them, particularly
in the present era of mass transportation and mixing of cultures.

It is generally possible to redefine any breeding population
as two or more smaller breeding populations. One of many ways
to accomplish this is to define two subcategories of the initial
population, one consisting of the higher-status people, and the
other consisting of the lower-status people. Since it is usually true
that men are more likely to marry (and to breed with) women
of about their own social status, these two subcategories of the
initial breeding population would each be a breeding population.
Many variables besides social status can be used to subdivide one
breeding population into two. Thus, ethnic groups are usually
breeding subpopulations of a multiethnic society. Within an
ethnic group the best-looking men and women may form a breeding subpopulation, and the most intelligent of the best-looking
(or the best-looking of the most intelligent) may form an even
smaller breeding subpopulation.

Geographic locales can also be used to define very small
breeding populations, since marriage tends to breed men and
women who have grown up in the same locale and who will raise
children in that same locale. Wales, for example, as small as it is,
may be divided into even smaller geographical areas which cor-

respond to meaningful breeding subpopulations. The major blood types (O, A, B, and AB), which are completely determined by three alleles (*A, B,* and *o*), have differing frequencies in these areas (Figure 5–1), indicating that different gene pools are associated with each area (Mourant and Watkin, 1952).

RACES

It should be clear by now that the number of separate breeding populations, or gene pools, that one wishes to recognize is arbitrary. The very largest meaningful breeding populations are usually referred to as *races,* and it is in the designation of races that this arbitrariness is most troublesome.

In 1775, Blumenbach made a fivefold classification of races, based on skin color, which has had remarkable influence: Caucasian (white skin); Mongolian (yellow); Ethiopian (black); American (red); and Malayan (brown).

However, skin color is obviously not the only trait in which people differ. Some people have straight and others wavy or curly or frizzy or peppercorn hair; some have prominent and thin and others broad and flat noses, thin or thick or everted lips; some are tall and others short or pigmy, some have long, others intermediate, and still others round heads, etc. If the variations in all these traits paralleled each other, race classification would be strengthened. But they frequently do not: for example, some people in southern India have very dark skin but straight or wavy hair, and the Bushmen of South Africa have peppercorn hair but yellowish skin. A race classification made on the basis of the hair shape would be different from that based on skin color or height or head shape (Dobzhansky, 1962:254).

Attempts to characterize races by a combination of these traits led to very large and arbitrary classification schemes. Because things quickly got out of hand, there was a move back to simpler classifications based on differences in gene frequencies (mainly blood genes) between population groups as well as on the traditional phenotype differences. Using blood type distributions, Boyd, in 1950, suggested a five-race classification consisting of European (Caucasoid), African (Negroid), Asiatic (Mongoloid), American Indian, and Australoid. These five correspond to the five inhabited continents and are similar to Blumenbach's original scheme, but this newer version is supported by blood tests. Subsequent schemes have begun to include more races again.

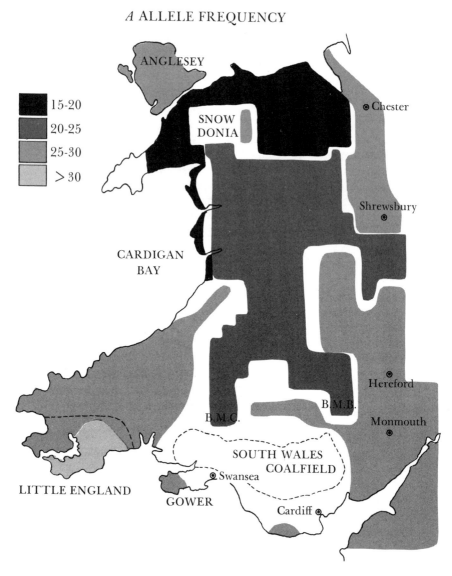

FIGURE 5–1.   Gene frequencies in Wales. (Mourant and Watkin, 1952:21, 25)

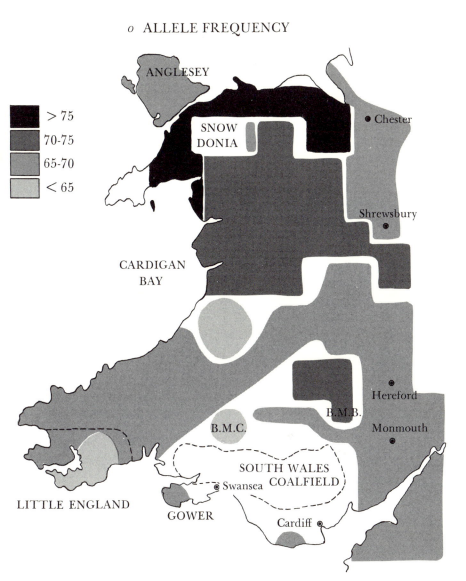

o ALLELE FREQUENCY

> 75

70-75

65-70

< 65

There is some disagreement as to just what these lists mean. Garn considers that there are thousands of "local races," and of these he has compiled a relatively small list of 32 which were selected because they were particularly well known or unusually interesting from a scientific or historical point of view; he does *not* consider the list a complete catalog (1971:169). Since 31 of the races in Dobzhansky's (1962) 34-race scheme are taken from Garn's list, Dobzhansky apparently *does* consider it to be a fairly complete catalog. We reproduce Dobzhansky's scheme here, maintaining that it is as good as any, since the best that can be hoped for is an intelligent, but arbitrary, listing of the most salient and/or relevant breeding populations.[1]

1. *Northwest European:* Scandinavia, northern Germany, northern France, the Low Countries, United Kingdom, and Ireland
2. *Northeast European:* Poland, Russia, most of the present population of Siberia
3. *Alpine:* from central France, south Germany, Switzerland, northern Italy, eastward to the shores of the Black Sea
4. *Mediterranean:* peoples on both sides of the Mediterranean from Tangier to the Dardanelles, Arabia, Turkey, Iran, and Turkomania
5. *Hindu:* India, Pakistan
6. *Turkic:* Turkestan, western China
7. *Tibetan:* Tibet
8. *North Chinese:* northern and central China and Manchuria
9. *Classic Mongoloid:* Siberia, Mongolia, Korea, Japan
10. *Eskimo:* arctic America
11. *Southeast Asiatic:* South China to Thailand, Burma, Malaya, and Indonesia
12. *Ainu:* aboriginal population of northern Japan
13. *Lapp:* arctic Scandinavia and Finland
14. *North American Indian:* indigenous populations of Canada and the United States
15. *Central American Indian:* from southwestern United States, through Central America, to Bolivia
16. *South American Indian:* primarily the agricultural peoples of Peru, Bolivia, and Chile

[1] Garn's original list, which forms the basis for Dobzhansky's scheme, appears in *Human Races* (1971), Charles C Thomas, Springfield, Illinois. Reprinted with the permission of Charles C Thomas, Publisher, and Stanley M. Garn.

17. *Fuegian:* nonagricultural inhabitants of southern South America
18. *East African:* East Africa, Ethiopia, a part of the Sudan
19. *Sudanese:* most of the Sudan
20. *Forest Negro:* West Africa and much of the Congo
21. *Bantu:* South Africa and part of East Africa
22. *Bushman and Hottentot:* the aboriginal inhabitants of South Africa
23. *African Pygmy:* a small-statured population living in the rain forests of equatorial Africa
24. *Dravidian:* aboriginal populations of southern India and Ceylon
25. *Negrito:* small-statured and frizzly-haired populations scattered from the Philippines to the Andamans, Malaya, and New Guinea
26. *Melanesia-Papuan:* New Guinea to Fiji
27. *Murrayian:* aboriginal population of southeastern Australia
28. *Carpentarian:* aboriginal population of northern and central Australia
29. *Micronesian:* islands of the western Pacific
30. *Polynesian:* islands of the central and eastern Pacific
31. *Neo-Hawaiian:* an emerging population of Hawaii
32. *Ladino:* an emerging population of Central and South America
33. *North American Colored:* the so-called Negro population of North America
34. *South African Colored:* the analogous population of South Africa (Dobzhansky, 1962:263–264).

The 34 races listed could have been combined into fewer races, or any of them could have been subdivided further. We must emphasize that these races are not totally endogamous; there is almost always some degree of cross breeding. In fact, 4 of the 34 races are direct results of cross breeding within the last 400 years.

The North American Colored race (33) arose from a mixture of races 20, 21, 1, 3, 4, and probably some others; the South African Colored (34) from 21, 22, 1, and 3; Ladino (32) from at least 15, 16, 4, 20, 21; and Neo-Hawaiian (31) from 30, 1, 9, and some 4, 8, and 11. Their recent hybrid origin makes these races no less real and natural than the others listed (Dobzhansky, 1962:265).

It is important to bear in mind that the geneticist's notion of race as a major breeding population with an associated gene

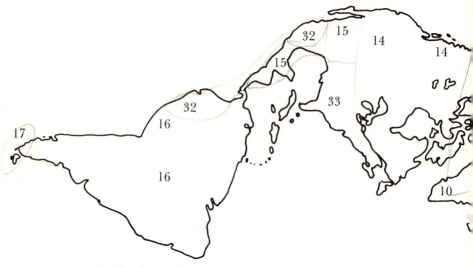

1. Northwest European	18. East African
2. Northeast European	19. Sudanese
3. Alpine	20. Forest Negro
4. Mediterranean	21. Bantu
5. Hindu	22. Bushman and Hottentot
6. Turkic	23. African Pygmy
7. Tibetan	24. Dravidian
8. North Chinese	25. Negrito
9. Classic Mongoloid	26. Melanesian-Papuan
10. Eskimo	27. Murrayian
11. Southeast Asiatic	28. Carpentarian
12. Ainu	29. Micronesian
13. Lapp	30. Polynesian
14. North American Indian	31. Neo-Hawaiian
15. Central American Indian	32. Ladino
16. South American Indian	33. North American Colored
17. Fuegian	34. South African Colored

FIGURE 5–2. The geographic occurrence of Dobzhansky's thirty-four races of man. (Dobzhansky, 1962:264. Reprinted with the permission of Yale University Press.)

pool is different from the common meaning of "race." Most people speak of races when they wish to differentiate large groups of people who *look* very different from each other; this may or may not infer that the groups have differentiable gene pools. Also, common usage frequently infers that one race is superior to another, and/or that there is enmity between the groups. These meanings attached to the term "race" have much relevance for the social scientist. In fact, they go a long way toward explaining why races tend to remain separate even when they are spatially contiguous. Biased racial attitudes serve as *isolating mechanisms* which inhibit interbreeding and the resultant mixture of gene pools.

The notion of isolating mechanisms is central to modern evolutionary theory.[2] Probably the most important isolating mechanism *between species* is the biological inability to form viable zygotes; but there are additional interspecies isolating mechanisms such as differences in preferred habitats, different breeding seasons, incompatibilities in physique and behavior which inhibit breeding, and an apparent simple lack of sexual attraction between species.

Since any man is biologically capable of breeding with any woman, the *within species* isolating mechanisms which separate human groups are either spatial or social in nature. Spatial isolation is a rather trivial mechanism, since physical proximity is obviously necessary for breeding (unless one wishes to consider artificial insemination). The social isolating mechanisms are much more interesting. We will not attempt a general treatment of them but will illustrate several with an example.

---

[2] In fact, Mayr defines speciation—the formation of new species—simply as "the acquisition of isolating mechanisms" (Mayr, 1970:323). One could probably argue from this definition that races, since they are isolated breeding populations, are separate species. We doubt that Mayr meant to infer that; we certainly do not. There is a substantial problem in defining just what is meant by the term "species." Usually it is implicitly taken to infer that a sperm from one species and an egg from another could not be combined to produce a fertile offspring. This sort of definition would clearly include all human beings in one species, but it presents classification problems for other animals since we have very little direct information on which animals can or cannot cross. We know which animals do and do not cross—which is a very different thing—and from that viewpoint Mayr's definition is appealing. The mule is the best known example of the offspring of two "species" (horse and donkey) which gladly cross when given the opportunity. Male mules are sterile, but female mules can and do produce offspring (Savory, 1970).

THE JEWS: EXAMPLES OF GENETIC ISOLATION

The history of the Jews is a puzzle which may be pieced together from many sources including the biblical account, which may be partly fictitious, and genetic data. Abraham and his son Isaac (assuming they are real historical figures) apparently lived about 4000 years ago in the present area of Iraq. Isaac's son Jacob (also called Israel) had twelve sons, and their descendants are said to have formed twelve tribes. It is tempting to associate the Israelites with the modern Mediterranean race of Dobzhansky's classification, but this is risky since the relation of present-day races to those of 4000 years ago is not clear. As we get further into this example it will become increasingly difficult to decide what race Jews do belong to, or if they constitute a race—or two races.

According to the biblical account, the patriarchs were endogamous, tending to marry their cousins. The genes of this founding family may be thought of as a tiny sample of the gene pool of the surrounding population. Undoubtedly there would have been some ways in which such a small sample differed from the larger gene pool, and so Abraham's children would be expected to reflect the genetic idiosyncrasies of the sample. Given sufficient endogamy, the *founder principle* of population genetics predicts that these idiosyncrasies would eventually differentiate the gene pool of Abraham's descendants from the gene pool of the surrounding population. Such a differentiation would have been exaggerated when Jacob and his family, numbering (according to the Bible) 70 men plus women, moved to Egypt about 1700 B.C. They were initially well received, and undoubtedly some intermarried. But the subsequent period of slavery must have minimized interbreeding, and by the time Moses is supposed to have led his followers out of Egypt (about 1300 B.C.), they must have constituted a relatively distinct gene pool.

After some years of wandering about the desert, the tribes conquered the land that is modern Israel. We may assume some interbreeding between the conquerors and the subdued, as there usually is some. However, there was not complete amalgamation, and this can be attributed to the invaders' unique religious culture—particularly their preference for religious endogamy—as well as to the usual status differences and hostilities between invader and invaded.

The tribes were politically unified under Saul, David, and Solomon, but there were internal difficulties, and after Solomon's death Israel split into separate northern and southern kingdoms. Assyria conquered the northern kingdom in 721 B.C., destroying or dispersing that portion of the gene pool. All succeeding history of the Israelites is of the southern kingdom of Judah, and so from that time on they are called Jews. It seems safe to assume that most recognizable groups of later Jews derive at least in part from the gene pool associated with this small southern kingdom.

Babylon conquered Judah about 590 B.C., carrying a large part of the captive population back to Babylonia. Thus begins the long period of Jewish dispersal which climaxed in 132 A.D., when Rome barred the Jews from their capital city of Jerusalem. They soon spread over most of the known world (Dimont, 1962; Epstein, 1959; Parkes, 1964).

Intermarriage goes hand in hand with assimilation, and so where there were high rates of intermarriage between the newly arriving Jews and the indigenous populations, the Jews ceased to be identifiable within a few generations. But several isolating mechanisms served to keep intermarriage rates relatively low in many places, and there the Jews maintained a separate minority identity.

Jews tended to settle together into their own communities. This sort of flocking is normally observed among minority groups submerged in a majority population, but in the case of the Jews it was reinforced by the requirements of Jewish ritual. Prayer meetings require at least ten men; kosher food must be available; children must attend Hebrew school; women must use ritual bath facilities at the time of menstruation. One family alone cannot maintain these practices; a community is necessary. Additionally, there was the religious requirement of endogamy: A Jew must marry another Jew. When intermarriage did occur, the child would be considered Jewish only if his mother were Jewish. It seems likely that the effect of this law was to keep the hybrid offspring of a Jewish man and Gentile woman out of the Jewish group, thus reducing the usually diversifying effect of interbreeding on a gene pool. Finally, the Jews rarely proselytized, and they went so far as to discourage potential converts. These factors must have allowed many Jewish communities to remain relatively separate from the surrounding Gentile population.

Of course, not all the social isolating mechanisms originated with the Jews. The Roman laws of Constantine began a long line of legislation banning Jewish-Christian intermarriage, although in this particular case only marriage between Jewish men and Christian women was forbidden (Dimont, 1962:155).

The enforced isolation of Jews into urban ghettos began in the 1500's, but this was a result of mechanisms both within and without the group. Prior to that time, the Jews voluntarily settled in their own urban neighborhoods. According to Dimont, they were proud of their areas and sometimes demanded that a king grant them a charter of rights to these desirable neighborhoods. Many nobles and other wealthy non-Jews preferred to live in the Jewish quarter. When the Roman ghetto was instituted in 1555, the Pope designated an already existing Jewish quarter. "His problem was not getting the Jews in . . . but getting the Christians out. They liked it there, and only successive turns of the Inquisitional screw forced them out. It took over a century before Rome's Jewish quarter became a hundred percent Jewish ghetto" (Dimont, 1962:247–248).

The effect of isolating mechanisms was not limited to separating Jews and Gentiles. The Jews themselves were isolated into subgroups, and one major division—that between the *Ashkenazim* and *Sephardim*—has resulted in genetic differentiation which is observable today in blood type distributions. This particular division was not a consequence of the usual in-group–out-group mechanisms: It came about as a secondary effect of the great conflict between Christianity and Islam. These two religions had little contact off the battlefield, and they effectively divided the world into two isolated regions. The Jews, who had previously spread over the known world, were separated and isolated into two subpopulations, one dominated by Christianity and the other by Islam. This, of course, had differential effects on the evaluation of Jewish culture in the two regions, and soon there were two separate Jewish subcultures.

Even when Islam diminished as a power, the Ashkenazi Jews of eastern and western Europe and the Sephardic Jews of southern Europe (mainly Spain), the Mideast, and North Africa, remained separated by cultural differences, including different languages. Ashkenazim developed, in addition to local vernaculars, Yiddish, which was a combination of Hebrew and early German. The Sephardim's parallel linguistic development led to Ladino, which was a combination of Hebrew and Spanish.

Cultural separation was reinforced by distance and also by the perceived superiority of one subculture over the other. The "heights" of the Ashkenazi and Sephardic subcultures roughly correspond to the "heights" of their dominating cultures. When

Islam was in flower Sephardic culture, particularly in Spain, was perceived as superior. More recently, however, the Ashkenazim of Europe have been perceived as culturally superior, while the Sephardic culture has been associated with the underdeveloped countries of North Africa and the Mideast [3] (Dimont, 1962; Parkes, 1964). While these two Jewish groups were separated, they each intermarried to some extent with the surrounding non-Jewish populations. The result has been the formation of two separate Jewish gene pools.

Genetic differences between Ashkenazim and Sephardim can be illustrated using blood allele frequencies derived from several Jewish populations. Figure 5–3 (adapted from Mourant, 1959) shows allele distributions of four Sephardic populations and thirteen Ashkenazi populations.[4] The separation of these two clusters is clear. The figure also illustrates that the Sephardim differ from corresponding non-Jewish populations in the same four North African countries. Note, however, that they are closer to these Gentile groups than the Ashkenazim are, which indicates some intermarriage between the Jews and non-Jews of North Africa.

Differences between Jews and non-Jews of Europe are not so clear. (European non-Jews are not illustrated in Figure 5–3.) This must be partly a consequence of intermarriage, particularly in western Europe. In the Netherlands, which has a long history of Jewish-Gentile harmony, there are no differences in A and B allele frequencies between Jews and non-Jews. Central and eastern European countries did not enjoy such good interethnic relations, however, and most of these countries' populations show substantial differences in allele frequencies, but the differences have no consistent direction. Although there is fair clustering for the Jewish populations, this is not so for non-Jews, which indicates relative isolation between the Christian populations of Europe.

Ambiguities in the meaning of "race" should be apparent at this point. The Ashkenazim share genetic characteristics with the surrounding European Christians as well as with the Sephardim. The Sephardim share genes with the surrounding Moslems. Who belongs to what race? Are there two Jewish races? To further com-

[3] Relatively small groups of Sephardic Jews moved from Spain to the Netherlands and England in the 16th and 17th centuries, and eventually to the United States. These groups maintained a superior social position relative to the Ashkenazim into the early part of this century.

[4] The major blood types (O, A, B, and AB) are completely determined by three alleles (A, B, and o) at one locus pair. Since the percentages of all alleles must add up to 100 percent, a population can be completely specified by the percentages of the A and B alleles alone.

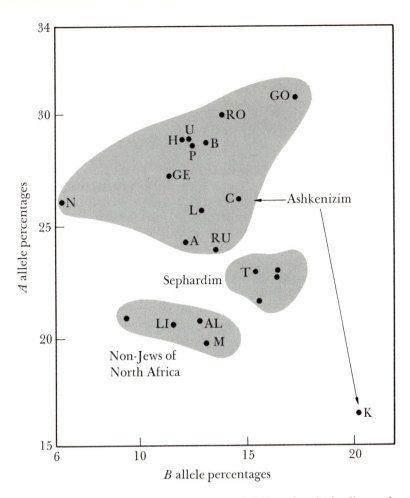

FIGURE 5-3. Blood allele percentages of Ashkenazim, Sephardim, and non-Jews of North Africa. (Adapted from Mourant, 1959)

Northern European Populations

A	Austria	L	Lithuania
B	Byelorussia	N	Netherlands
C	Czechoslovakia	P	Poland
GO	Georgia	RO	Romania
GE	Germany	RU	Russia
H	Hungary	U	Ukraine
K	Karaites		

North African Populations

AL	Algeria	M	Morocco
LI	Libya	T	Tunisia

plicate matters, there are genetic grounds for differentiating small populations of Kurdish and Persian and Iraqi Jews from the Sephardim and Ashkenazim (Lerner, 1968:172). Perhaps the best resolution of these difficulties is to abandon the notion of "race."

As more comparative genetic data become available from the many Jewish populations now gathered in Israel, we should get a clearer picture of their past migrations and mergers. The addition of genetic and linguistic data to traditional written forms of information opens a vast field of historical social research. Genetic data have already cleared up a few historical problems. Comparison of blood allele frequencies of Hungarians, Hungarian Gypsies, and Indians (from India) show the Gypsies to be much more similar to the Indians than to the Hungarians, indicating Gypsy roots near India which earlier had only been suspected because of the similarity between Gypsy language and Sanskrit.

We may soon have techniques for blood typing dead bodies; thus allowing investigations of gene frequencies in extinct populations. Perhaps we may then solve the intriguing puzzle of the Etruscans, whose culture contributed so much to the rise of Rome. Historians presently have little knowledge of how their culture evolved or from where they came (Lerner, 1968:228–230).

The degree to which foreign genes are allowed to enter a pool is probably the major reason for hereditary changes in human populations. There are, however, other sources of variability. Genetic material which is already present may be changed through mutation or by a recombination of genetic information.

Another source of variation within an isolated population is random *drift*. A child receives only half of each parent's genes. Just which genes are passed on is a matter of chance. Over a few generations, some genes may be passed on frequently, purely by chance, while others are hardly passed on at all. In a small population, this sort of randomness can be a major source of variation.

Then there is *selection*. Here, some nonrandom factor makes one sort of genotype reproduce more frequently than another. The "selected-for" genotype eventually becomes common in the gene pool, while the "selected-against" genotype becomes rare. Selection is one of the central notions of evolutionary theory. If a population is somehow divided into two isolated parts, and if for some reason different genotypes are selected for in each new population, two different gene pools will evolve. Presumably, the populations may eventually diverge to the point where they are no longer capable of interbreeding, and there would be two species where before there was one. In our opinion the mixing of gene pools through interbreeding is at present a much more important cause of human variation than selection. Nevertheless, selection constantly recurs as the conjectured mechanism which "explains" differences in human populations. Therefore, a more detailed examination of that process follows.

SELECTION

One of the best documented examples of genetic selection is Kettlewell's study of "industrial melanism" (reported in Ehrlich and Holm, 1963:125–131). During the past 120 years, dark (melanic) forms of camouflaged moths have appeared in many industrial areas. Estimated censuses of *Biston betularia* moths in the area of Manchester, England, indicate that in 1848, the melanic form of the moth made up no more than 1 percent of the moth population, but by 1898 it made up more than 99 percent of the population. Melanism is usually produced by a single dominant gene. The spread of the dark forms seems to be related to the soot pollution of woodlands around industrial areas. It has been hypothesized that in sooty woods the melanic forms are less visibie to predators than the typical light mottled forms, whereas in unsooted woods the typical form is better camouflaged. With the spread of industrial pollution, the melanic forms thus enjoy an increasing advantage which has allowed their genotype to predominate. This hypothesis becomes particularly appealing when one examines photographs of the two forms on an unpolluted, lichen-covered tree and on a soot-covered tree. To the human eye the theoretically proper moth is nearly invisible in each case, while the other moth stands out as a succulent target. Of course, human beings are not the moths' major predator, and as appealing as the explanation may sound to us, it must have empirical support to be accepted. Three lines of investigation do provide that support: 1) There is a strong correlation, in time and space, between industrialization and the increase in melanic forms. 2) Equal numbers of melanic and light moths were experimentally released in an unpolluted wood, and birds were observed to eat more of the melanics than the light moths. In a polluted area, the opposite was true. 3) Known numbers of each form were marked and released in polluted and unpolluted areas. Samples were then recaptured using a light. More melanics were recaptured in the polluted areas, and more of the lighter moths were recaptured in the unpolluted areas.

While the hypothesis appears to be confirmed, another line of investigation points to a very different explanation of industrial melanism. Under certain types of physiological stress, such as starvation, the larvae of the melanic form are better able to survive than the larvae of the lighter forms. Perhaps industrial pollution affected the moths' food supply—pollution is known to be harmful to some forms of vegetation—and under the stress of starvation the melanic larvae were favored. This would certainly explain the observed increase in darker forms. Perhaps both explanations are true. On the other hand, perhaps both of these mechanisms had relatively minor effects, and the real explanation of industrial melanism is unknown.

Selection arguments, particularly as applied to human groups, seem to be characterized by this sort of ambiguity. For instance, it has been argued that a red-green colorblind individual would be at a selection disadvantage in a hunting and gathering society, but not in a modern urban society (Post, 1962, 1963). Presumably, colorblindness inhibits hunting and gathering activities. Indeed, it turns out that in populations of Eskimos, Australian aborigines, and other hunters and gatherers, there is only a 2 percent frequency of red-green colorblindness among males, whereas in groups somewhat removed from hunting and gathering (American Indians, African Negroes) there is a 3 percent frequency, and in populations still further removed (Europeans, Filipinos, some Arabs) there is a 5 percent frequency of red-green colorblindness. But there are all sorts of differences between primitive and modern cultures, of which the practices of hunting and gathering are only two. Why should it be those differences which account for the data? One could undoubtedly pass an afternoon on feasibility arguments as to why other differences would do just as well. (See, e.g., Neel and Post, 1963.) Then the evening could be whiled away on cultural differences which would give the opposite results; e.g., the existence of traffic lights would put a red-green colorblind person at a disadvantage in modern society.

A reasonable selection argument can usually be constructed to explain any set of data. Dark-skinned people tend to live in climates with strong sunshine, while lighter-skinned people live in cooler or cloudy climates. This may be explained as an adaptation to ultraviolet solar radiation, protective coloration in tropical rain forests, or optimal vitamin D production (Dobzhansky, 1962:271–273; Lerner, 1968:231–233). If Negroes were lighter than Europeans, that could be explained by the fact that lighter skin reflects larger amounts of heat than darker skin, making light skin adaptive in a very hot, sunny climate. The relative beardlessness of Eskimos may be explained as an advantage because of the icicles that would form on the beard (Lerner, 1968:232). If Eskimos had beards, that might be an advantage because it would help keep their faces warm.

Gottesman (1968) has reviewed the interesting investigation of declining human intelligence through selection. Several studies indicated that parents with low IQ tend to have more children than parents with average or high IQ. This differential reproduction should have the effect of lowering the average intelligence level of the species. But large-scale IQ surveys taken 15 years apart failed to document this expected decline; in fact, mean IQ increased slightly. The paradox was resolved when further studies showed that a relatively large number of people with low IQ remain unmarried and childless. That is, when they *do* marry, they have many children, but they often do not marry. On the other hand, average- and high-IQ adults have fewer children *per marriage,* but they almost all marry. Taken on the whole, average- and high-IQ adults seem to be outproducing low-IQ adults, and the species is saved for the moment. But, we are already seeing signs of a new round of theorizing which assumes that it is mainly high-IQ college-educated people who are accepting the current "zero population growth" ideology of self-limitation on child production, and so the fate of the species may be in danger (Wallich, 1970). All this assumes, of course, that the distribution of IQ's in a population has an effect on its fate, which may not be the case.

Selection theories reach an apex of untestability when they aim to explain performance differences *between* groups. For example, one theorist explains the relatively high intellectual attainments of Jews by assuming that throughout the Middle Ages the most intelligent men—both Jewish and Christian—went into religion as their life's work. While priests were celibate, rabbis were considered ideal mates. Thus, "the fundamental reason for the observed differences is that Jewry bred selectively for intelligence during centuries in which Christendom bred selectively against it" (Weyl, 1966:2). The present authors (50 percent of whom are Jewish) find such arguments unappealing. Its correctness is not at issue; we have no way of testing whether it is true or false. It enjoys the philosophical convenience of being untestable. That in itself would not be so bad—there is nothing wrong with conjectural theorizing—except that *selection* conjectures lend themselves so readily to notions of biological superiority and inferiority

(Chapter 1). What is one to do but make equally untestable counterarguments: A 2,000-year *cultural* emphasis on universal education for males and the value of learning might better explain the intellectual attainments of Jews.

Even theorists who specifically disdain selection arguments to explain racial differences in IQ still use that form of argument to explain social class differences (Eckland, 1967; Gottesman, 1968). The social class argument assumes that mobility in an American-type society is partly tied to intellectual ability. Intelligent men tend to be upwardly mobile, and unintelligent men are downwardly mobile. The net effect should be an embarrassment of genetic riches in the upper-class gene pool. The argument sounds all right, but given the limitations of our present methodology, it too seems to be untestable. The fact that upper-class children score relatively high on IQ tests is no proof. Cultural factors which differentiate the upper and lower classes could easily account for test-score differences. This is the ubiquitous hooker in every biological argument which "explains" behavior differences between breeding populations. Any group that shares a gene pool also shares a culture. Genetic transmission and cultural transmission both follow similar interpersonal pathways. Therefore, almost any difference between breeding populations which might be genetically "caused" might also be culturally "caused." At the present time there seems to be no way of analyzing these "causes" separately.

As long as our selection theorizing must stay in the realm of the relatively untestable, we may accept or reject these explanations on the basis of ideology rather than on the basis of evidence. If we are committed to the "equality" of social classes, we could argue that the upper class is not disproportionately accumulating "intelligence genes" because the theory does not take into account large immigrations, such as those into the United States during the first half of this century. Many of these migrants came from middle class backgrounds and/or from countries where they had limited mobility opportunities. Financial and language difficulties and limited job opportunities here forced most of them to enter the American working class. This suggests a large enough infusion of intelligent genes into the lower class to counter the postulated mobility effect. We have, of course, no way of evaluating whether there was a net gain or loss to the lower class gene pool.

This becomes a pointless exercise in cleverness, since we cannot make the necessary empirical tests. We can, of course, throw out really bad arguments if they are grossly out of line with whatever data are available. But in general, with our present methodological limitations, we cannot demonstrate that behavioral differences between two breeding populations are genetically based. Neither can we prove the contrary.

Jensen (1969) recently made an assault on the methodology problem in his controversial analysis of Negro-white IQ differences. His strategy roughly was this: We can agree that if two breeding populations differ in their distribution of blood phenotypes, this difference must be genetically based because culture has no apparent effect on blood. Similarly, if we could show that culture has relatively little effect on IQ, then large differences between races are unlikely to be due to differences in cultural environments. Therefore, they are more likely to be due to genetic differences. We will come back to this argument, but first we must consider what it means to say that the cultural environment has "relatively little effect" compared to the genes. This begins to sound like older notions of the relative importance of heredity versus environment.

HEREDITY VERSUS ENVIRONMENT, REVISITED

At one time there was considerable debate about whether heredity or environment was more important in determining an individual's characteristics. Today we consider that a naive question. An individual's characteristics (his phenotype) must develop; they do not appear full-blown in the newborn. Heredity (the genotype) is the necessary beginning point of development. Environmental influence is necessary to sustain the organism; an unnurtured infant will die. Since both are necessary for the individual's development, it is rather meaningless to ask what is more important.

Some have made an unwarranted extension of this newer thinking. They dismiss all quantitative comparisons of heredity and environmental effects as meaningless. Actually, some such comparisons can be both meaningful and useful. Consider the following examples:

All individuals have one of four types of blood: O, A, B, or AB. These blood types are completely determined by one locus pair of the individual's genotype. One of three gene alleles may occur at each locus. These alleles are denoted *A, B,* and *o.* If the individual's pair of gene alleles is *AA* or *Ao,* he will have type A blood; if the pair of alleles is *BB* or *Bo,* he will have type B blood: if the allele pair is *AB,* he will have type AB blood; and if the pair is *oo,* he will have type O blood. Thus, the genes completely determine the blood type. Differences in environment seem to have no effect. That is not to say that heredity is more important for blood than environment is. Without environmental interaction the individual would die, and there would be no blood at all. But variation in the genotype (i.e., in heredity) is more important than environmental variation in accounting for differences in blood type.

Now consider the characteristic of IQ. In the last chapter we saw that IQ was largely dependent on heredity, but it is also abundantly clear that a child's IQ can be altered by exposing him to more or less stimulating environments. Environmental variation is more important in accounting for variations in IQ than in accounting for variations in blood type.

We should be able to order several characteristics in a similar way, starting with those like blood type, on which environmental variations have *no* apparent effect; moving through characteristics like intelligence, on which environmental variation has *some* effect; and concluding with those like length of haircut, on which environmental variations (i.e., haircutting) account for *all* variation in the characteristic. Figure 5–4 is just such a list. The criterion for ordering used here is the intrapair correlation for monozygotic twins who have been raised apart. We have used the

Figure 5–4. Intrapair correlations for identical twins reared apart.*

Characteristic	Approximate correlation
Blood type	(1.00)
Height	.82–.96
IQ	.75–.87
Weight	.37–.88
Scholastic achievement	.60–.76
Introversion-extraversion	.61
Neurotic tendency	.53
Length of haircut	(.00)

* The two values enclosed in parentheses have not actually been measured in twin studies but are assumed to be true. They have been included to extend the list of correlation values to its theoretical limits. The other values were obtained from Newman, Freeman, and Holzinger, 1937; Shields, 1962; Erlenmeyer-Kimling and Jarvik, 1963; and Burt, 1966. All of these values are based on studies of white populations in Europe and America.

following reasoning: If the members of a monozygotic twin pair are raised in different environments, they should grow up to be most different on those characteristics which are most subject to change under environmental variation. Therefore, the intrapair correlation of a characteristic should be an inverse measure of that characteristic's environmentally induced variation. The higher the correlation, the less effect environmental variation had on the characteristic. Thus, the correlation betwen monozygotic twins who have been raised apart should be higher for IQ than for length of haircut.

In interpreting Figure 5–4, two essential points must be kept in mind. First, the values were obtained from studies of twins in white American and European populations. These cultural environments are very different from, say, Japanese cultural environments or the social environments which we may some day see in special schools. There is no compelling reason to think that correlations obtained from a population in a very different culture (or a different population in the same culture) would give the same values we have here. Twin studies from China might give a very different ordering of characteristics. *Any such ordering has meaning only for the population in which the correlations were obtained.*

The second point is a corollary of the first. Since the correlation for any characteristic is a function of the particular population, it cannot be an intrinsic property of the characteristic. *Therefore, a high correlation does not necessarily indicate that the characteristic has an intrinsic resistance to environmental influence.* For example, the .9 correlation for height is very high, but it does not mean that height is intrinsically resistant to change from environmental factors. We have already pointed out that American-born offspring of Mexican and European migrants grow up to be taller than their parents, apparently because of differences in American diets (Chapter 4). This is an extreme environmental influence on height. It is not reflected in the .9 correlation because that value was calculated from twins in similar environments *within* America. Had one twin from each pair been raised in America and the other in Mexico, the correlation would undoubtedly have been much lower.

Since for a particular culture, or a particular population, different characteristics have differing degrees of variability caused by the environment, it becomes meaningful to ask what portion of the *total observed variability* within the population is due to environmental variations within the culture, and what portion is due to heredity differences within the population? Geneticists have defined *heritability* (*H*) as that portion of the total observed population variance which is attributable to heredity differences. This is a newer way of looking at the old question of heredity versus environment. Note that we are no longer asking the question about individuals, but about *populations* of individuals.

THE TROUBLE WITH "HERITABILITY"

When we measure a quantitative characteristic like IQ for all the members of a population, it is customary to summarize the data by calculating the *mean* and *variance* of all the values. "Variance" is simply a convenient statistical measure of the variability of the characteristic within the population. The total observed variance (V_o) may be divided into variance attributable to heredity (V_h) and variance attributable to environment (V_e).[5] This is expressed as

$$V_o = V_h + V_e.$$

Dividing through by V_o, we get

$$1 = \frac{V_h}{V_o} + \frac{V_e}{V_o} = H + E,$$

in which *H* denotes the proportion of the observed variance due to heredity, and *E* denotes the proportion due to environment. *H* is the "heritability." Its value may range from zero, when none of the variance is due to heredity (as in length of haircut), to one, when all the observed variance is due to heredity.

Note that heritability is similar to the twin coefficients of the last section because it, too, is as much a function of the particular population as the particular characteristic. An estimate of the heritability of a characteristic calculated from data from one population is not necessarily generalizable to different populations.

Although heritability is certainly a theoretically meaningful population concept, in practice it is difficult to separate the genetic and environmental sources of variance. One laboratory procedure applicable to fruit fly population involves the reduc-

[5] In this simple treatment we are ignoring the variance due to interaction of heredity and environment, and error variance.

tion of hereditary variance until it is negligible. First, the variance of the characteristic is observed in a normal population in a "normal" environment. Call this observed variance V_{o1}. Then the variance of the same characteristic is observed in a highly inbred population raised in the same environment. Call this V_{o2}. If the inbred members are assumed to be almost identical genetically, then V_{o2} must be almost entirely due to the environment. The difference between the two observed variances must be due to hereditary variation in the normal population; so that

$$V_h = V_{o1} - V_{o2}.$$

The heritability of the original normal population is then obtained by dividing V_h by V_{o1} (Ehrlich and Holm, 1963:52–53). The heritability of the inbred population is, of course, almost zero.

Such laboratory methods are not applicable to human beings. There are, however, several statistical techniques currently in use for estimating the heritability of characteristics for human populations. All these methods are based on questionable assumptions (Falconer, 1960; Vandenberg, 1968; Wright, 1969; Crow, 1969). They involve correlation of the characteristic in question among relatives who share a known proportion of genes. (For example, monozygotic twins share all their genes; dizygotic twins and other siblings, as well as parent and child, share 50 percent of their genes; first cousins share 25 percent of their genes, etc.) But since the degree to which genes are shared is related to the degree to which environments are shared, it is difficult to partition the genetic and environmental contributions. The most common approach is to compare monozygotic and same-sex dizygotic twins on the assumption that two children of the same age growing up in the same house will be subject to the same variation in environmental influences. The differences between monozygotic twins will be purely environmental, while differences between dizygotic twins will be the result of the same magnitude of environmental variation *plus* a 50-percent difference in genes. Therefore, it should be possible to separate the genetic and environmental differences.

Smith (1965) has tested this assumption by correlating twins on characteristics which seem unlikely to have any genetic component, e.g., time of getting up in the morning, dress, and study habits. In general, monozygotic twins showed higher correlations than same-sex dizygotic twins, indicating that there may be different environmental variances acting. Sandra Scarr (1968) has argued that if parents treat identical twins more similarly than dizygotic twins, that may be more a *result* of the similar behavior of the monozygotic twins than a cause of it. She presents only minimal empirical support for that position, however. On the other hand, there is also evidence that some parents of identical twins may go out of their way to differentiate them, with the result that identical twins living apart are sometimes more similar than identical twins living together (Wilde, 1964). At the present time, any calculation which assumes equal environmental variation for monozygotic and dizygotic twins is suspect.

One way out of this difficulty is to study a population made up of monozygotic twin pairs, each of which had been separated at birth, so that the twin mates were raised in very different environments. Call the total observed variance of the characteristic V_o. V_o would be the result of both hereditary and environmental differences within the population. The variance *within* twin pairs (V_e) is due solely to environment, since each pair of twins is genetically identical. Then, if we subtract the variance due to environment alone (V_e) from the variance due to both heredity and environment (V_o), we get the variance due to heredity alone. Therefore,

$$H = \frac{V_o - V_e}{V_o}.$$

If this expression is rewritten in terms of the intrapair correlation for the monozygotic twins raised apart (r_{MZA}), we get, simply,

$$H = r_{\text{MZA}}.$$

Then the values of r_{MZA} in Figure 5–4 may be used as estimates of H for white populations in Europe and America.

There are still difficulties with this analysis. It assumes that the twins were raised in widely varying environments. In fact, twins who have been separated early in life are usually placed in homes which are fairly similar, and so the values of H obtained this way are deceptively high because part of the correlation which we attribute to genetic similarity is actually due to environmental similarity. In one IQ study, Burt (1966) was able to locate twins who had been separated into widely varying home environments, but his value of .87 for r_{MZA} is higher than the average value of .75 (Erlenmeyer-Kimling and Jarvik, 1963) obtained from studies of separated twins who were raised in more similar environments. These results suggest that there are unresolved problems with this methodology.

Although the concept of heritability is meaningful, we feel that the practical difficulties in applying it to human populations are substantial. In addition, the concept is frequently misused and misinterpreted. Earlier in this chapter we mentioned Jensen's attempt to investigate the basis of Negro-white IQ differences. He tried to show that the heritability of IQ is very high ($H \approx .75$), thus demonstrating that intelligence variation has a large genetic component. Jensen then claims that it is reasonable to hypothesize that Negro-white IQ differences have some genetic basis (1969:82). It should be clear by now that even if we assume that the estimate of IQ heritability among white Americans and Europeans is correct, and even if a similar high value of H could be shown to characterize the American Negro population, we still could not say that white-Negro differences are genetically based because the environmental variation *between* the white and Negro populations might be large enough to account for the differences. The IQ situation may be analogous to our earlier example of American-born offspring of Mexican and European immigrants. Height has a higher heritability than IQ (according to estimates from white American and European populations). Yet the children of these immigrants grew taller in the new environment than their parents did in the old environment. It seems likely that a similar increase in IQ would occur in Negro children if they moved into white middle-class environments. We agree with Jensen that the genetic hypothesis cannot be summarily dismissed. But neither do we have any good reason to seriously entertain it at the present time.

CONCLUSIONS

The ideas of population genetics, which have been fruitful for our understanding of biological evolution, can also aid our understanding of contemporary human social groups. Certainly the definitions (and difficulties in definition) of "racial" and "ethnic" groups take on a new clarity in this context, and that alone would justify the inclusion of these ideas in social science.

Unfortunately, some of the concepts which have been useful in examining plant and animal populations may be counterproductive when applied to human beings. We have focused on problems associated with "selection" and "heritability." Selection theorizing, which so easily lends itself to the old racist ideas of biological superiority and inferiority, is usually not testable in human populations. Therefore, selection theories which "sound very good" usually cannot be empirically refuted or confirmed. We do not advocate that such theorizing be banned, but we do urge that before any theory is taken seriously the theorist should specify some reasonable empirical test which would allow its rejection. Race problems are sufficiently acute without exacerbating them with quasi-scientific theories of biological advantage.

Heritability, like selection, is a concept for which the disadvantages of misuse may outweigh the advantages to be gained from its proper application. We are wary of the negative consequences which may result from the uncritical application of these population genetics notions to contemporary social science.

Suggested Reading

Mankind Evolving, by the eminent geneticist Theodosius Dobzhansky (Yale University Press; New Haven: 1962), is a highly readable account of the evolution of human populations.

For a complete modern treatment of the subject of race, see S. Garn's *Human Races* (Charles C Thomas; Springfield, Ill.: 1971).

One of the clearest treatments of mathematical methods of population genetics is D. Falconer's *Introduction to Quantitative Genetics* (Ronald Press; New York: 1960).

CHAPTER 6   HORMONE SYSTEMS

THE PRECEDING CHAPTERS HAVE EMPHA-
sized the effects of biological attributes on social behavior. The
genes contain directions for the building of cells, organs, and
organ systems and set limits on their growth and function. The
effects of genes on behavior are indirect, being accomplished
through the constructed biological attributes. The day-to-day
functioning of these biological attributes is not just a consequence
of genetic instructions, however; they also depend on stimuli
from the physical and social environment. It is at this level that
most of the interaction between the biological and the social
environment occurs, with effects in both directions: biological on
social and social on biological. This chapter outlines some current research in the interaction of the nervous system, the hormone system, and the social environment, emphasizing the possible consequences of these interactions in the onset of some
diseases.

Determining the relationships among the nervous system,
the hormone system, and the social and physical environment of
the human organism is one of the more challenging problems of
investigation and knowledge synthesis facing modern scientists.
The term "hormone" refers to several types of substances which
are transferred throughout the body by the blood stream (Brown
and Barker, 1966). Hormones are produced by cells located in
various parts of the body, usually in the ductless glands known
as the endocrines which are shown in Figure 6–1. There are few
cells and no organs or organ systems which are not, at one time
or another, affected by one or more hormones. Propositions re-

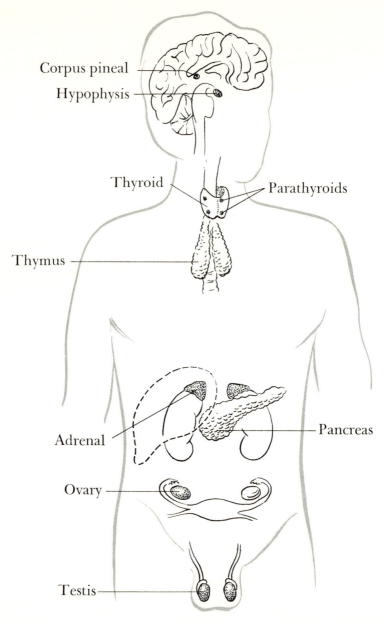

Corpus pineal

Hypophysis

Thyroid

Parathyroids

Thymus

Adrenal

Pancreas

Ovary

Testis

FIGURE 6–1. The major endocrine organs of the human male and female. The function of the pineal and the thymus as endocrine glands is a matter of some controversy and is not discussed in the text. The terms hypophysis and pituitary refer to the same gland (Brown and Barker, 1966).

garding their function are essential to an understanding of the organism's behavior and its interaction with other organisms. Since some hormones affect the secretion of other hormones either directly, through chemical action at the cellular level, or indirectly, through the nervous system, the notion of an overall balance or "homeostasis" (Cannon, 1932) has long been associated with the interactions of hormones and other body systems. These interactions are so complex, however, that only a few variables are investigated in any one research project. Therefore, an overall model which demonstrates all the factors maintaining or disrupting homeostasis remains to be constructed (Mason, 1968a).

NEUROHORMONE SYSTEMS

Homeostasis occurs through an unknown number of interlaced feedback systems. "Negative feedback" occurs when an initial action results in a second action or chain of events which at some point results in a decrease in the initial action which precipitated the chain. For example, a dog barking in the night may awaken a lady who wakes up her husband who calls his neighbor who quiets the dog. If there is not a negative [1] link in the chain of events, the initial action and its results will be maintained at a higher or increasing level. Such a chain is called "positive feedback." For example, if the husband in the above example curses the neighbor who beats as a scapegoat the dog whose louder and louder barking angers the wife who asks her husband to call again and so on, there is no negative relationship to reduce the barking. Also, the other neighbors are soon likely to enter into the process.

By carefully following the arrows in Figure 6–2 which displays some known relationships among the nervous system, endocrine systems, and metabolic systems, one can see that there are many feedback relationships. Known positive or negative effects are indicated by the direction of the arrows. Arrows to the left of the solid line show the adrenal-cortical system. Through a com-

---

[1] A "positive relationship" among phenomena occurs when an increase in A results in an increase in B, or a decrease in A results in a decrease in B. An increase in A resulting in a decrease in B, or a decrease in A resulting in an increase in B is called a "negative relationship." See Coleman (1964, 1968) and Stinchcombe (1968) for excellent discussions of the use of mathematics to study feedback systems. Much of the original thinking on the effects of feedback on biological and social organization is found in a collection of articles edited by Buckley (1968).

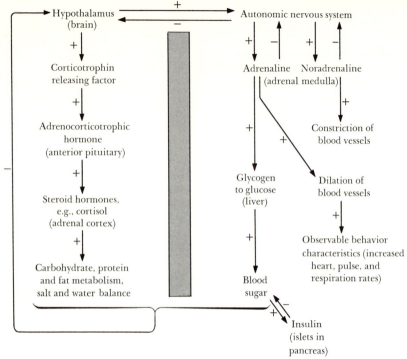

FIGURE 6–2. Greatly oversimplified schema of some relationships among nervous systems, hormone systems, and metabolic systems.

plex sensory process the brain monitors the need for protein, salt, water, etc. The brain maintains a balance among these elements by stimulating the release of adrenocorticotrophic hormone in the anterior pituitary gland which in turn affects the release of steroid hormones in the adrenal gland. The level of the steroid hormones in the blood as well as their effect on metabolism, salt and water balance, and other body functions are in turn monitored by the brain.

Perhaps the most observable results of hormone action (other than those of the sex hormones or gross abnormalities such as goiters) are the increased heart, pulse, and respiration rates affected by the release of adrenaline. As shown in the subsystem displayed to the right of the solid line in Figure 6–2, both adrenaline and noradrenaline are released from the adrenal medulla, the core of the adrenal gland. Adrenaline dilates the blood vessel system producing the externally observable actions just mentioned (i.e., increased heart, pulse, and respiration rates) while noradrenaline constricts peripheral blood vessels. Adrenaline has particularly wide-ranging effects. For example, it is known to inhibit ovulation, probably because of its effect on the part of the brain which controls hormones in the anterior pituitary gland which, in turn, affects the sex glands. Noradrenaline has fewer directly observable effects but it is known to be important in the transmission of nerve impulses, being secreted at various nerve endings as well as in the adrenal gland. Any of the hormones may also have effects which are as yet unknown.

Since there is interaction of elements within the brain as well as interaction of elements at the metabolic level, these subsystems are also interrelated. Not only must the elements within a subsystem be balanced but the relative secretions of the subsystems must be balanced in a complex interplay of one against another. Figure 6–3 gives a more detailed picture of the site of action of just those hormones secreted by the anterior pituitary.

Many think the term "hormone" is synonymous with sex, but actually only a few hormones are directly related to sexual functioning. The interest in them is indicative of the importance of sexuality in human relations. In most mammals, the male is prepared for sexual relations from puberty until old age without seasonal variation. In primates, and particularly in man, sexual activity is found beyond the decrease in gonadal secretions in the aged (or when the gonads are surgically removed), apparently because needs other than the satisfying of a visceral drive are served by sexual relations. Frequency of sexual relations is more often controlled by the female and is at least partially determined by seasonal or monthly cycles in secretion of the gonadotrophic hormones from the anterior pituitary.

Figure 6–4 displays the stages of the ovulatory cycle and the action of various hormones at each stage. In the nonpregnant female, the cycle begins after menses when the brain releases a substance which stimulates the anterior pituitary gland to secrete follicle-stimulating hormones (FSH). Growth of the immature egg cell in the follicles is affected by FSH. The maturing cell produces estrogen and the amount of estrogen in the blood is monitored by the brain which regulates the relative amounts of FSH and luteinizing hormone (LH) produced by the anterior pituitary. The relative balance of these hormones is important in the maturing of the egg. When LH is secreted at a given level, the egg is released into the uterus. Progesterone is added to the estrogen produced by the egg and the preparation of the uterus for pregnancy begins. However, if the egg is not fertilized by sperm from the male, progesterone and estrogen secretion declines, the uterus expels the preparatory material (in menstruation), and the decrease in progesterone and estrogen is monitored

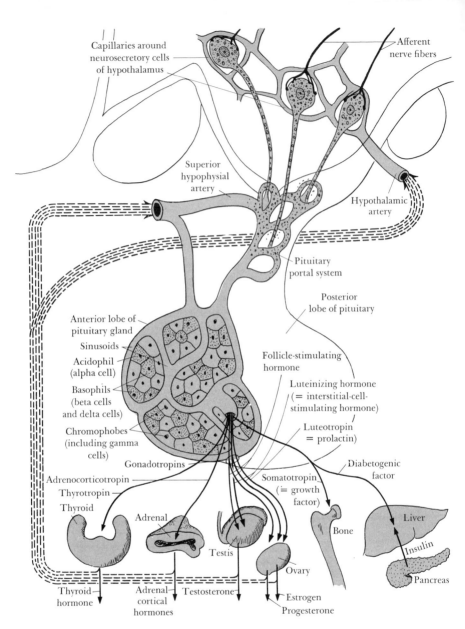

Capillaries around
neurosecretory cells
of hypothalamus

Afferent
nerve fibers

Superior
hypophysial
artery

Hypothalamic
artery

Pituitary
portal system

Posterior
lobe of pituitary

Anterior lobe of
pituitary gland

Sinusoids

Acidophil
(alpha cell)

Basophils
(beta cells
and delta cells)

Chromophobes
(including gamma
cells)

Gonadotropins

Adrenocorticotropin

Thyrotropin

Thyroid

Follicle-stimulating
hormone

Luteinizing hormone
(= interstitial-cell-
stimulating hormone)

Luteotropin
= prolactin)

Diabetogenic
factor

Somatotropin
(= growth
factor)

Adrenal

Testis

Ovary

Bone

Liver

Insulin

Pancreas

Thyroid
hormone

Adrenal
cortical
hormones

Testosterone

Estrogen
Progesterone

FIGURE 6–3. Circulatory flow between the hypothalamus, and anterior
pituitary gland, and other organs. (Copyright 1965 CIBA Pharmaceutical
Company, Division of CIBA Corporation, reproduced with permission from
THE CIBA COLLECTION OF MEDICAL ILLUSTRATIONS by Frank H.
Netter, M.D.)

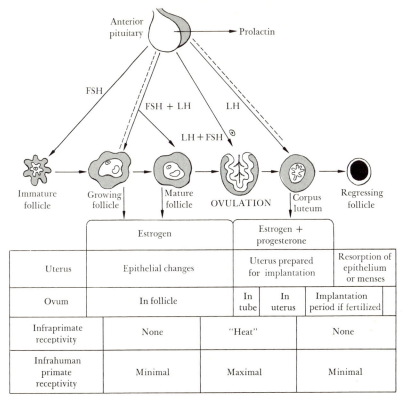

FIGURE 6-4.   Sequence of events in the ovary and uterus during the estrus or menstrual cycle. (From C. T. Morgan, *Physiological Psychology*. Copyright 1965 by McGraw-Hill, Inc. Used with permission of McGraw-Hill Book Co.)

in the brain where FSH releasing factor is produced to restart the cycle (Morgan, 1965).

HORMONES AND BEHAVIOR

In most mammals the female is receptive to sexual advances by the male or, in some cases, is herself sexually aggressive, only during a short period in the estrus cycle (Figure 6-4). Primates show less well-defined time periods of sexual activity but the frequency is definitely higher at mid-cycle in monkeys and apes. A recent report of human sexual intercourse indicated a peak "near mid-cycle, a fall early in the luteal phase and a secondary premenstrual rise" (Michael, 1968). Thus, the high level of estrogen produced by the ovaries at mid-cycle probably influences sexual desire in the female (Morgan, 1965). However, human sexuality is also highly influenced by symbol systems. Although there may not be as much "sexual meaning" in as many symbols as some Freudian theorists would have us think, there is certainly much interaction of symbolic and physical systems in human sexual arousal.

Other changes in psychic states have been correlated with the menstrual cycle. The "blues" reported by many women in the days before menstruation and the depression often experienced after childbirth both occur at a time when progesterone is reduced (Hamburg et al., 1968). Over half the suicides attempted in a sample of female psychiatric patients occurred either in the four days preceding or during menstruation (Dalton, 1959). Since sex hormones do not operate independent of the other hormones or of behavior systems, no such findings can be attributed to one factor.

In addition, of course, the effects of heredity on the activity of the neuroendocrine system must be included. The structure of the glands is determined by directions from the genes, and individual variation in genetic effects on some glands is well known. For example, diabetes, which is a result of insufficient insulin secretion from the islets of the pancreas, is primarily caused by a recessive gene. In sex differentiation, the presence of the Y chromosome apparently determines the production of androgen at a crucial point in the development of the embryo, and thus male sex characteristics are developed. "The principle of differentiation somewhat simplified appears to be: add androgen and obtain a male . . . add nothing and obtain a female" (Money and Ehrhardt, 1968). What is known about the evolution of the endocrine systems is a fascinating story (Barrington, 1964) but it is too long to tell here.[2]

Whatever the genetically determined balance of the hormones within or between species, they are quite sensitive to social and physical stimuli (Mason and Brady, 1964). Animal experiments indicate that a certain amount of such stimulation is necessary to activate the balanced systems (Levine, 1960; Schaefer, et al., 1962; Hutchings, 1963; Brauer, 1965; Denenberg, 1970). Once homeostasis is established relative to the type of stimula-

---

[2] The story of Adam and his rib is more charming but the evidence indicates that it did not happen that way.

tion to which the animal is accustomed, marked changes in stimulation may be too severe for the organism to change to new adaptive levels. This may explain why young children, deprived of their mothers and reared in foundling homes where they receive minimal stimulation, have a high frequency of physical, emotional, and social problems as well as a high death rate (Spitz, 1965).

The effects of stimulation on an animal may be contingent on genetic factors. King and Eleftheriou (1959) compared mice from a strain described as wild and emotional with a strain described as docile and found that handling over time decreased the performance on a conditioned task of the wild emotional strain but increased the performance of the docile strain on the same task. In sum, animals of like genetic background react differently given differential stimuli at critical points in the maturation process, and animals of different genetic backgrounds react differently to the same stimuli.

The specific interactions of hormones and social stimulation have been investigated in a few species including man, but the results are not conclusive. Since there are such wide varieties of species, body systems, and social situations to be investigated, it is not surprising that relatively few systematic interspecies comparisons have been made. Therefore, the degree to which findings are species specific usually cannot be assessed. That caution is in order when generalizing findings from one species to another is illustrated by differential relationships among hormones where comparisons have been done. For example, adrenaline has no effect on the secretion of growth hormone in man or squirrel monkeys, but it has a strong effect in the rhesus monkey (Reichlin, 1968). Nevertheless, it is instructive to review a few findings to understand the enormous potential for research in this area.

Perhaps the simplest illustration of the role of social stimuli is the association of crowding, social rank, and the size of adrenal glands of various animals. The weight of these glands is indicative of their activity. It has been shown that adrenal weight increases in size in direct proportion to the density of the population in mice, wild rats, wild deer, and monkeys (Mason, 1968b). In rats and mice the weight of the adrenals is related to the number of fights they have lost, indicative of subordinate status (Barnett, 1955). Indeed when mice which have been consistent losers in fights are placed in the presence of successful fighters, their adrenocortical activity is as pronounced as that found during actual fights (Bronson and Eleftheriou, 1964).

Injection of adrenaline or noradrenaline in mice has been shown to affect dominance in obtaining food (Lawrence and Haynes, 1970). After being deprived of food for 24 hours, pairs of mice were started from equidistant points and arrived at a point where one had to squeeze the other out to obtain food. Noradrenaline injections increased dominance while adrenaline injections decreased dominance as compared to situations in which the mice received no hormone injections.

No clear theory of the interplay of social dominance and physiology has emerged to explain these findings. Why is it that monkeys who are usually harassed by a dominant partner show improved body needs for certain elements (cholinasterase, calcium, and serum protein) [3] when placed in isolation? (Angermeier, et al., 1968). For human beings we understand these processes even less although it is clear that there exists some sort of relationship between human physiology and factors related to status. Kasl, et al., (1970) recently summarized a group of studies relating various indicators of achievement to levels of uric acid (related to gout) and cholesterol (related to some forms of heart disease) in the blood. Controlling for IQ, persons with high grade-point averages in high school tended to have higher uric acid levels and lower cholesterol levels than persons with intermediate or low averages. Persons with high uric acid also saw more difficult jobs as more attractive and showed less test anxiety. These associations were strongest when cholesterol was low. Cholesterol levels were negatively correlated with high school grades. Kasl and his co-authors rightly concluded that more research is needed before definitive conclusions are reached.

Another researcher showed that persons with particular discrepant social statuses manifest a greater number of psychosomatic symptoms including nervousness, shortness of breath when not exercising, rapid heart beat, and sweating hands, which are indicators of an adrenalinelike reaction to stress. Persons with high *ascribed* status (such as a white Anglo-Saxon Protestant) but low *achieved* status (such as low education or occupation) reported significantly greater numbers of such "symptoms" than those who had equal ascribed and achieved statuses, or low ascribed and high achieved status (Jackson, 1962). It appears that, in man, it is not just subordinate status but the type of subordinate status that affects physiologic systems. When lack of achievement cannot be blamed on low status ascribed by society, the

---

[3] These substances are not hormones but they strongly interact with hormones in metabolism.

individual may be punitive toward himself or at least inhibit aggressive tendencies which arouses the emergency mechanisms of the body.

Hormone reaction to *stressors* has been studied more frequently than has the correlation of hormone patterns with other behaviors because of the possibility that some diseases are linked to stress through hormone reactions. We shall turn now to the secretion of adrenaline and noradrenaline under stress because they have been more thoroughly studied than the other hormones and because of their interesting behavioral manifestations.

SOCIAL CORRELATES OF HORMONE REACTION TO STRESS

Adrenaline and noradrenalinelike reactions to stressors are related to a person's verbalized emotional response and to his pattern of relationships with parents. Funkenstein, et al., (1957) measured heart and blood vessel reactions in [4] students placed in two stressful situations. In one situation, the students were asked to tell a story. Each student's voice was delayed slightly on a tape recorder and played back to him through earphones; this usually causes stammering. A mild electric shock was administered when stammering began. The second stressful situation involved the solution of arithmetic problems without benefit of pencil and paper while the experimenter made caustic comments when incorrect answers were given. Interviews with the subjects after exposure to each of the situations revealed that their emotions could be classified into one of three categories: anger toward the experimenter or a scapegoat, anger toward themselves, or anxiety. Furthermore, those with anger toward others tended to show a noradrenalinelike physiological response, and those with self-anger or anxiety more often showed an adrenalinelike response.

Subjects who reported before the experiment that their fathers were distant and authoritarian while their mothers were

[4] Since blood or 24-hour urine samples are necessary for direct assessment of hormone levels, in human experiments it is often necessary to use indirect indicators such as heart and pulse rates (Funkenstein, et al., 1957). Each of these measures presents advantages and disadvantages. Indirect indicators are relatively easily obtained, but one cannot be sure that a given hormone is causing the reaction measured. Hormones in urine may be diluted relative to their volume at their site of action. The stress of taking a blood sample can affect the volume of some hormones (Mason, 1968).

affectionate were more often in the anger-out group. Those in the anger-in group more often said that both parents shared authority and were warm and affectionate. The anxious group, however, had missing or "Casper Milquetoast" fathers, their mothers being the source of both discipline and affection.

Funkenstein and his colleagues interpreted their findings by concluding that a distant and authoritarian father would be an attractive target for a child's aggressiveness. The child could presumably aim all his attacks at this father with no fear of losing affection since the father did not supply affection anyway. This child then becomes used to directing anger at another person (his father), and as a grown man he will continue the pattern of expressing anger at others. On the other hand, a child who receives both discipline and affection from the same source—either from both parents or from just the mother—will be inhibited from expressing aggression at the source of authority since by doing so he may lose his source of affection. This child must inhibit his aggression with the result that he will either turn his anger in at himself or experience anxiety.

A straightforward interpretation of Funkenstein's results would say that different hormones cause different emotions; that noradrenaline causes the emotion of anger toward others, and adrenaline causes the emotions or anger toward self, or anxiety. That this is not the case was amply demonstrated by Schachter (1964) who showed that one hormone, adrenaline, could contribute to two very different emotions: anger and euphoria. Schachter told subjects that he was studying the effects of a vitamin which would be injected into them. Actually the "vitamin" was adrenaline. One group of subjects was told there would be certain side effects: shaking hands, pounding of the heart, and a warm flushed face. These are the normal effects of adrenaline, so these subjects were correctly informed of what to expect, and they will be designated the "adrenaline-informed" group.

A second group of subjects was also told of side effects, but they were given an incorrect list of symptoms to expect: numb feet, itching. These subjects are designated the "adrenaline-misinformed" group. A third group was told nothing about side effects and will be called "adrenaline-uninformed." A fourth group was given a "placebo" injection which has no effect on the body and they too were told nothing of side effects.

Each subject was introduced to a stooge and told to wait with him for several minutes. When the experimenter left the room, the stooge went through a prearranged act, being either very happy and euphoric in one condition of the experiment or very angry at the experimenter in another condition. The subjects were observed during this interaction, and afterward they were questioned about their emotions.

The results can be summarized as follows: Whatever the emotion of the stooge (euphoria or anger), the adrenaline-uninformed subjects were more likely to show signs of that emotion than the placebo subjects. (Therefore adrenaline contributes to two very different emotions.) Whatever the emotion of the stooge, the adrenaline-informed subjects were the least likely of all subjects to show signs of that emotion. Furthermore, in the "euphoria" condition, the adrenaline-misinformed subjects showed the greatest euphoria.[5] These results indicate that emotions do not have single causes. The observed emotional behavior was a joint function of the adrenaline, the expectations that subjects were given about the adrenaline, and the cues they received from the stooge. A substantial amount of work must still be done for us to gain a complete understanding of these relationships.

One of the present authors has speculated that adrenaline and noradrenaline responses to stress may explain some relationships between perceived parental characteristics and affiliative behavior (Robertson and Dotson, 1969). High school students in this study answered questions about their relationships with their parents and the number of extracurricular activities in which they participated (the latter being taken as a measure of affiliation). It was expected that students with more expressive parents would be more dependent and, therefore, more affiliative. However, this was true only for first-born students who reacted to a stressful task in an adrenalinelike fashion. Those first-borns who reacted with a noradrenalinelike response showed more affiliations when their parents were nonexpressive. While the latter finding continues to puzzle us, it is clear that the effect of parental expressivity on affiliation is contingent upon hormonal response to a stressor.

In the case of the adrenalinelike response, it may be that the highly affectionate parents display their affection most often when they can see that their child is distressed, that is, when his response to stress is adrenalinelike. (Remember that the adrenaline response—shaking hands, warm flushed face—is much more visible than the noradrenaline response.) If such displays of affection increase dependency, and dependency results in affiliation (which

---

[5] Schachter did not anticipate this interesting result and so he did not run adrenaline-misinformed subjects in the "anger" condition.

is yet to be proved), then the results for those who react in an adrenalinelike fashion are explained. Such dependency may contribute to his being a "joiner" later in life. The fact that the results were not found among the later-born does not mean that later-born children are any less loved by their parents, but they probably receive less attention because, with their arrival, parenthood is no longer unique, and the parents must divide their attention among two or more children, and undoubtedly older children have an effect on the behavior of young children.

A STRESS THEORY OF ILLNESS

While the relationships between physiological reaction to stress, emotional responses, family relationships, and affiliation must be further researched, our present knowledge allows for some interesting speculation on their possible role in stress-related disease. Too much or too little hormone secretion is thought to be an important factor in the development of a number of diseases. For example, there is a relationship between concentration of blood cholesterol and coronary artery athrosclerosis. The amount of cholesterol in the blood plasma is related to the degree of secretion of a number of hormones (Back and Bogdonoff, 1964). Funkenstein et al., (1957) report excessive levels of adrenaline in schizophrenics and noradrenaline in paranoids. Some other chronic diseases are also known to be related to excessive or insufficient steroid levels (Selye, 1956).[6]

The basic question underlying these findings is: Why are the hormones sustained at a level outside their normal limits? We have seen that normal limits are maintained by negative feedback systems. If positive feedback occurs, the elements of the system are no longer balanced. It is quite possible that some positive feedback systems come into operation through the relationship of

[6] It should be noted that a number of factors, genetically and otherwise determined, may also be important in the etiology of a given disease and one cannot attribute it to one "cause." It is the interplay of various factors over an extended period of time which puzzles the scientist trying to understand them and frustrates the therapist trying to manage them.

The portrayal of the psychiatrist's couch where discovery of a single traumatic event in the life of the patient leads to cure of the neuurosis or psychosis is misleading. A single event may be illustrative of an overall set of life experiences but it has not been shown that a single event "causes" emotional or physical problems, if indeed they can be separated, or that discovery of such an event leads to a "cure."

hormone balance to social affiliation, thus creating the conditions for one or another of these illnesses.

Do different people respond differently to too little (or too much) social affiliation? The Dohrenwends (1966) have shown that subjects isolated in a sensory deprivation experiment showed differential stress symptoms depending on their birth order. First-born children were highly stressed by isolation while later-born children were not. The opposite reaction was found for people living in crowded slum conditions. Later-born persons in such situations reported more stress symptoms than did first-born persons. So first-borns appear to be most stressed by too little social affiliation, and later-borns are more likely to be stressed by too much affiliation. Furthermore, we know that when first-borns are stressed they tend to seek social affiliation; however, this is not true of later-borns (Schachter, 1959).

It may be that the sustained hormone levels observed in certain types of illness are affected by two types of positive feedback systems. When a person (e.g., a first-born) who tends to need affiliation is socially isolated, he is stressed and his affiliation needs are amplified. If he is unable to find social interaction to satisfy the affiliation needs, he is stressed further and the cycle repeats itself with an accompanying sustained hormone level. A similar chain may occur for the nonaffiliative person; that is, stress increases the need to be alone, but the person's life situation demands intense social interaction which further increases his need to be alone, and so on. Should such a process continue, an illness may result depending on the hormones involved, genetic propensities, diet, etc. (Kosa and Robertson, 1969). Such a theory implies that it is not just hormones, birth order, or personality needs which result in chronic disease, but that it is the "fit" among these factors and the social environment that is of primary importance.

While hardly proving or disproving the theory, some studies have shown pathological physiological patterns to be related to marked decreases in social affiliation. LeShan (1966) found the following life pattern in 70 percent of terminal cancer patients studied: "Childhood and adolescence marked by feelings of isolation; a sense that intense and meaningful relationships are dangerous and bring pain and rejection; and a sense of deep hopelessness and despair" followed in adulthood by a meaningful relationship with one person and finally "loss of the central relationship in a sense of utter despair, and a conviction that life held nothing more for them." Only 10 percent of a control group without cancer reported a similar pattern. Of course, it is possible that the despair reported by the cancer patients is a result of knowledge of impending death rather than the loss of their "central relationship." However, comparison of mortality rates in a number of studies have shown that the widowed have mortality rates from cancer about four times that of those who are married at the time of death (LeShan, 1966). Cancer is, in this view, related to the loss of a close person or relationship.

Again, the cross-species jump from human beings to rats is large and must be taken with care, but it is interesting to note that mammary tumors develop considerably less frequently in multiple caged rats than in rates caged alone (Brauer, 1965). Such tumors are known to be related to hormone reactions, and one group of researchers, after demonstrating such relationships, stated "host response to the mammary tumor agent, i.e., the development of mammary cancer, is determined by hormonal factors. Thus the host response is dependent not only on factors directly or indirectly acting on the mammary tumor agent as such, but also on those factors acting on the endocrine system" (Muhlbock and Boot, 1960).

CONCLUSIONS

This chapter began by pointing out that internal control of various body functions is usually thought to be the result of the interaction of various hormone systems, metabolism, nervous systems, and the brain. It is clear from the studies of these systems that a complete biological model of the human organism must also include inputs to and from the social environment. Although the model is not yet complete, it appears that a certain amount of social stimuli, depending on the species, is necessary to activate not only the nervous system but also the hormonal systems at certain critical stages in their development if the organism is to adapt to such stimuli at a later point of life.

A certain level of stimulation is also necessary to maintain these systems at their usual levels. For example, the adrenal gland atrophies and becomes incapable of producing necessary levels of steroids if the hormones are provided artificially over too long a period of time. And, as we have seen, sustained stress with the accompanying sustained imbalance in hormone levels may result in disease or lower resistance to disease-producing agents. The longer a stress occurs in time, the greater the probability that permanent damage will be done by the overcompensation of those systems necessary for adaptation. Positive feedback—arising out of an interplay between personality needs, social environment, and physiological reaction—is hypothesized as a particular case of long-term stress which is likely to have damaging effects. We expect that further research on these notions will be rewarding both in terms of basic knowledge of the interaction of soma, psyche, and social environment as well as increased knowledge of the origins of the so-called stress diseases.

Suggested Reading

J. H. U. Brown and S. B. Barker provide a lucid discussion of hormones in their *Basic Endocrinology* (F. A. Davis; Philadelphia, Pennsylvania: Second Edition, 1966).

A volume edited by R. P. Michael, *Endocrinology and Human Behavior* (Oxford University Press; London: 1968) includes a number of articles by prominent researchers studying hormones (mainly sexual) and behavior.

One of the classic studies of hormonelike reactions to stressors in relation to family background and relations with peers is *Mastery of Stress* (Harvard University Press; Cambridge, Massachusetts, 1957) by Daniel H. Funkenstein, Stanley H. King, and Margaret Drolette.

Detailed bibliographies on the relationships of hormonal and behavioral systems are found in an entire issue of *Psychosomatic Medicine* (30:565–808, 1968) by J. W. Mason and colleagues.

CHAPTER 7   SOCIALIZATION

THERE ARE PITFALLS IN GENERALIZING FROM
chickens to humans since their differences go well beyond the
discrepant use of eggs. Yet, many theorists see the "imprinting"
phenomenon of chickens and other fowl as a model of early
human socialization (Gray, 1958; Scott, 1962; Ambrose, 1963),
and therefore imprinting is an interesting topic with which to
begin this chapter.

IMPRINTING

A newly hatched chick will follow almost any moving object
and behave as if that object were its mother. Usually the object *is*
its mother and things work out nicely, but if the experimenter
arranges for an abnormal first encounter—substituting for the
mother a bird of a different species, or a human being, or even
a moving ball—the chick will attach itself to that object. Ducklings
that have been imprinted on decoys will not follow a live mallard
female. In fact, they will avoid her and move closer to the decoy
(Hess, 1959). A bird that is abnormally imprinted may avoid associations with species mates and have abnormal sexual relations
when adult, directing its sexual attention to objects which are
similar to its imprinting object.

In rigorous studies of imprinting, birds are hatched and
maintained in darkness and isolation until, at the appropriate
time, they are exposed to a moving decoy or some other imprinting
object (Hess, 1959, 1962). Each baby is then tested to see the effect
of the imprinting exposure. The baby birds are given four oppor-

tunities to approach either the imprinting object or some roughly similar object. The percentage of positive responses are then recorded for each baby. A positive response to the imprinting object on all four tests is regarded as complete, or as 100 percent imprinting. The top graph in Figure 7–1 shows the average score for chicks exposed to the imprinting object in different age groups (solid line). Some imprinting occurs in newly hatched chicks, but maximum scores occur in chicks who are 13 to 16 hours old at the time of exposure. These hours are considered the *critical period* for chickens. If the chick has not been imprinted by that time, the likelihood of successful imprintation becomes increasingly small.

It should be noted that the literature is mainly concerned with animals who are imprinted to abnormal objects and does not describe the subsequent development of animals who pass through their critical period without being imprinted at all. In considering the possibility of imprinting in human beings, we must distinguish between a baby imprinted to a nonhuman object and a baby who is not imprinted at all. There are so called "feral children" who are supposed to have been nurtured by wolves, but reports of such children are of doubtful authenticity (Ogburn and Bose, 1959; Lorenz, in Kuhlen and Thompson, 1970:46). The relevant problem for human beings concerns the baby who is not imprinted at all during its critical period. Until recently, infants reared in orphan institutions experienced very little prolonged human contact during their first year of life. This sort of social deprivation during the child's critical period could presumably inhibit imprintation. We will examine some data on institution-reared children, but before that, we will note some interesting results on chicks' development of fear responses.

Chicks in several age groups were exposed to a decoy, just as in the imprinting experiment. A chick who emitted distress notes in the presence of the decoy or moved away from it was considered to have shown fear. The percentage of chicks in each age group who showed fear of the potential imprinting object is plotted (dashed line) in the top graph of Figure 7–1. Very young chicks show no fear of the decoy. It is only toward the end of the critical period that fear responses build up. Hess (1959, 1962) notes that the onset of fear will prevent an unimprinted animal from engaging in the kinds of social behavior which are necessary for imprinting to occur. Therefore, the onset of fear should mark the end of the critical period. Hess hypothesizes that all animals showing the phenomenon of imprinting will have a critical period that ends with the onset of fear and suggests that we can predict the

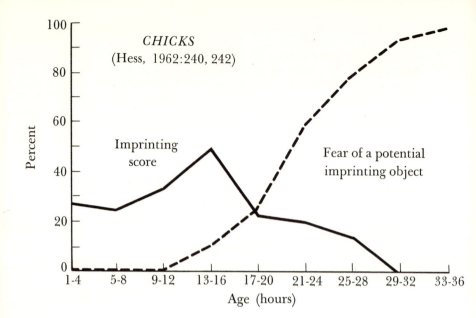

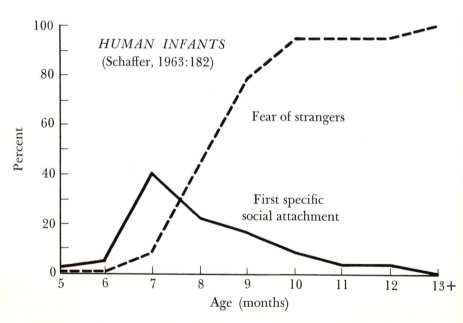

FIGURE 7–1. Social attachment behavior and fear behavior, in baby chicks and baby human beings.

end of imprintability in any species if we know the time of onset of the fear response in that species.

The second graph (dashed line) of Figure 7–1 shows the onset of fear of strangers in human babies. We have used Schaffer's (1963) data from a group of 23 babies, plotting the percentage of that group who showed fear by each age.[1] Onset begins about six months of age and increases through the first year (Morgan and Riccuiti, 1969). Schaffer also tried to measure the age at which babies form their first attachment to a specific other person. Toward this end, he studied each baby's response to separation situations which occur in everyday life—when, for example, the infant is left alone in a room, or when he is put down after a period on an adult's knee. Schaffer determined the age at which each baby began protests directed at a specifiic individual in these separation situations. The percentage of the group which thus showed a first specific social attachment is plotted as a function of age (solid line) in the second graph of Figure 7–1. The peak period for first social attachments is seven months of age.

Schaffer's test of infants has substantial similarity to Hess's imprinting test of chicks. In both cases the babies were first exposed to a "social" object, then deprived of it, and then given a chance to respond to the lost object. In both tests the babies were scored for responses toward the lost object. On the basis of these analogous graphs for chickens and human beings, if there is a critical imprinting period for human beings, then we would guess it to be at the age of seven months.[2]

One could test the hypothesis that human beings imprint by removing three groups of babies from human contact for a fixed period of time. One group (the experimental group) would be isolated during the hypothetical critical period, and the other two control groups' periods of isolation would bracket the critical period. If the hypothesis is correct, the subsequent development of the experimental group babies would be more abnormal than either of the control groups. We obviously do not care enough about testing the hypothesis to seriously consider such an experiment, but there are some "natural experiments" which have inadvertently occurred as the result of the social deprivational condi-

---

[1] The two "fear" plots are not fully comparable because a new group of chicks was used at each age while the same group of human infants was used for all the data points.

[2] We reemphasize the words "if" and "guess" in this sentence. Gray places the human critical period for imprinting between six weeks and six months (1958:161).

tions which existed in many orphanages until recently. Skeels describes care of babies in one of these institutions in the 1930s:

Until about 6 months (of age), they were cared for in the infant nursery. The babies were kept in standard hospital cribs that often had protective sheeting on the sides, thus effectively limiting visual stimulation. . . . Human interactions were limited to busy nurses who, with the speed born of practice and necessity, changed diapers or bedding, bathed and medicated the infants, and fed them effectively with propped bottles.

Older infants, from about 6 to 24 months, were moved into small dormitories containing two to five large cribs. This arrangement permitted the infants to move about a little and to interact somewhat with those in neighboring cribs. . . . The children had good physical and mental care, but little can be said beyond this. Interactions with adults were largely limited to feeding, dressing, and toilet details (1966:3–4).

If the imprinting hypothesis is correct, children who experienced this social isolation in institutions during the critical period (about seven months of age) should show more abnormal development than children who were isolated before or after (but not during) that period. We have examined the published data, limiting ourselves to studies which followed up subjects at least into adolescence. Four studies appear to be relevant:

Skodak and Skeels (1949) report that the IQ scores of a sample of 100 adolescents who had been placed in adoptive homes under the age of six months were somewhat above average.

Goldfarb (1943) studied a sample of 15 adolescents who had lived in an institution prior to entering foster homes. At least twelve of them had been in the institution during the critical period. Compared with a control group of adolescents who had always lived in foster homes, the institution children had lower IQ scores, were emotionally more apathetic, were withdrawn in their social relationships, and had substantially more behavioral problems.

Goldfarb (1947) did another study of 30 adolescents who had been adopted after spending some time in child institutions. Fifteen of these subjects had been admitted to the institution under the age of six months and were institutionalized during their critical periods. Seventy-three percent of these were judged to have made poor social and emotional adjustments during adolescence. The other 15 subjects were admitted to the institution after the age of six months, most of them after the age of seven months. Only 27 percent of this group were judged to be poorly adjusted.

Skeels (1966) reports on 13 subjects who entered regular child institutions and then were transferred (as part of an experiment) to the intensive care of older women inmates in a mental hospital. Eleven of these children were subsequently placed in foster homes, and a follow-up study indicated that all had made normal life adjustments as adults. With one possible exception, these subjects initially entered the child institution well after the critical period.

These four studies are all consistent with the imprinting hypothesis. Children who leave the institution before the age of seven months or who do not enter until after that age usually develop normally. Children in the institution at the age of seven months are more likely to show abnormalities. There are, however, alternative explanations of these findings. The abnormal or poorly adjusted children generally have had longer tenures in institutions than the normal children.[3] It is not clear if a long tenure is more of a cause or an effect of abnormal adjustment. In any case, the imprinting hypothesis is in no sense proved.

Using the primate series (Chapter 2) may provide an adequate and ethical test. Although we cannot do imprinting experiments on human beings, we can do them on other primates. In fact, the Harlows (1962) have done such an experiment by raising rhesus macaques in isolation for a period of time and then letting them enter into social interaction with peers. Monkeys who were isolated for the first 80 days of life developed normal behavior after being allowed several months of play with peers. Monkeys isolated for the first six months of life or longer did not normalize. These results suggest the existence of a critical period somewhere between the third and sixth month of life during which social deprivation, particularly deprivation of the company of peers, harms the animal's capacity for social adjustment. These results could be refined and similar experiments run on chimps, squirrel monkeys, and the other primates of the series. If it were demonstrated that these primates do indeed have critical periods for imprinting, and if these periods progressed through the series in an orderly manner (say, squirrel monkeys: one month; macaques: three months; chimps: six months), there would be a compelling case for the existence of imprinting in human beings.

[3] Spitz (1965: Chapter 14) has shown that when good mother-infant relations existed before separation, the length of separation is strongly related to depression and physical deterioration in the infant.

One final word on critical periods—if one exists, then several may exist. We have already reviewed the evidence of a critical period for the acquisition of language, running from age two years to puberty (Chapter 3). Scott (1962) has suggested that human beings have different critical periods not only for imprinting and language acquisition but also for each behavioral and physiological phenomenon. At this point we are over our heads in speculation, so we will reenter firmer ground. We move now to a consideration of the effects of a person's physique on his socialization.

PHYSIQUE

It is convenient to think of three ways in which physique can effect socialization: (1) Ego's physique may alter the probabilities that he will enter one social group or another. A tall boy is more likely to join the basketball team than a short boy; a pretty girl is more likely to be frequently dated than a plain girl. (2) Once in a social group, physique will affect ego's form of interaction. The first meeting of a handsome young man and a pretty girl will be qualitatively different than the first meeting of that same man and a homely girl (Walster, et al., 1966; Byrne, 1968). The pretty pair will be more flirtatious, more ingratiating, and more pleasant to each other. We may expect the pretty girl's self concept to develop along rather different lines from the homely girl's. (3) Ego tends to accept cultural values associated with his type of physique and to evaluate himself accordingly. He will be proud of a "good" physique and ashamed of a "bad" one.

These three effects will now be examined in greater detail, starting with the manner in which physique may alter the probabilities of ego entering one group or another. The example of the tall boy and the basketball team is trivial, and if we can carry the effect no deeper than that it will be useless. Our more complex illustration is drawn from Skipper and McCaghy's study of stripteasers. Their 35 subjects had outstanding physiques. Compared with average American women of comparable age and even to Playboy Playmates of the month, "the strippers were taller, heavier, with larger hips, and had extremely well-developed busts, several approaching astronomical proportions" (1970:6). Their careers cannot be explained simply on the basis of physique, however. These additional factors were common in the majority of subjects: 89 percent of the girls were the first-born child in their family; at least 60 percent came from broken and unstable homes; almost all reached puberty at a relatively early age; many had early coital experience (at least 25 percent before age 15 and 75 percent before age 20); an unusually large number broke their family ties by the age of 18, usually through marriage.

Several studies indicate that first-borns are more likely than later-borns, to seek social affiliation when they are under stress (Schachter, 1959; Sampson, 1965). These girls, coming from broken homes in which they received little attention and affection, must have felt strong unfulfilled affiliation needs. Their early puberty brought substantial physical attraction, and Skipper and McCaghy conjecture that the girls began to use their bodies to gain attention and to meet affectional needs. One girl recalls:

Sure, after I bloomed I always dressed so people could see how big my breasts were. After all, a pair of 48's can make a girl feel like a real person. Everybody pays attention (1970:9).

This appears to have led directly to early coital experiences and early marriage.

The emphasis on body and exhibitionism which began at puberty carried through. Prior to becoming strippers, over 70 percent of the girls had such jobs as go-go dancer, artists' model, or hat-check girl, where body display is a major feature of the occupation. Very few had seriously considered stripping until shortly before their first performance. Entry into the profession usually occurred when the girl was in economic need and an acquaintance suggested that stripping was lucrative. Since stripping requires little or no training, the final step was quite easy. The girl's arrival as a stripteaser was facilitated by her sexy physique, but this was clearly only one of several interacting factors which increased the probability that she would enter that particular career group.

Once in a group, physique may alter a person's form of interaction. Consider first Goffman's analysis of interaction between a physically abnormal (stigmatized) person and a physically normal one:

[T]he stigmatized individual . . . will have special reasons for feeling that mixed social situations make for anxious unanchored interraction. But if this is so, then it is to be suspected that we normals will find these situations shaky too. . . . Each potential source of discomfort for him when we are with him can become something we sense he is aware of, aware that we are aware of, and even aware of our state of awareness about his awareness; the stage is then set for . . . [an] infinite regress of mutual consideration. . . . [I]t is understandable that all will not go smoothly. . . . And since the stigmatized person is likely to be more often faced with these situations than are we, he is likely to become more adept at managing them (1963:18–19).

A person's physical abnormality may have more reality in his mind than his body, particularly in adolescents who experience major bodily changes with very little accompanying understanding of just what is going on. Some teenage boys temporarily accumulate fat around the hips, thighs, and nipples, and they perceive that they are following a feminine growth pattern which is a cause of substantial discomfort and disadvantage in peer interaction. Among adolescent girls, tallness and fatness appear to be the main foci of perceived abnormality. Dwyer and Mayer (1968) studied obesity in a population of high school students and found that while only 16 percent of the girls were obese and presumably should be dieting, about 30 percent were actually on diets at the time they were questioned. In contrast to the girls, 19 percent of the boys were found to be obese, but only 6 percent were on diets at the time of questioning.

In high school, peers are very important; a large portion of a girl's popularity is based on her looks, and much of a boy's popularity is based on looks and athletic skill (Coleman, 1963). The student's self concept must be effected by success or failure in peer interaction, and that must in turn depend partly on physical attractiveness and, in boys, physical skill as an athlete. Early maturers of both sexes tend to be taller and have larger body builds than their slower-developing classmates. For boys, early maturation would appear to be an advantage since it gives them an edge in sports and in height over their girl classmates, and, additionally, it gives them the prestige of shaving. Empirical results do indeed show that early-maturing 17-year-old boys are more self-confident while later-maturing boys of the same age tend to have negative self concepts and to feel inadequate (Mussen and Jones, 1957). Jones (1957) followed up a sample of early- and late-maturing boys when they were 33-year-old men. By this time the physical differences between the two groups had largely disappeared; however, there were some personality differences which appear consistent with adolescent differences. The men who had been early maturers were now more dominant, more likely to be consulted for advice and reassurance, more self-controlled, more willing and able to carry social responsibility, and had made successful vocational adjustments. In contrast, the men who had been late maturers appeared to be more dependent, rebellious, impulsive, self-indulgent, and more likely to have made poor vocational adjustments. In brief, the late physical maturers appeared to be less psychologically mature as men (although they were also more insightful). It is not clear from these results whether late physical maturers never quite reach the same level of psychological maturity as early physical maturers or whether they are simply slower to mature, even at the age of 33.

Using a similar logic for girls, one would guess that early maturation would be a disadvantage since it would mean that the girl was taller and heavier than most of her classmates (Frisch and Revelle, 1970). But empirical results show early-maturing girls to have more favorable self concepts than late-maturing girls. On the other hand, late-maturing girls have higher prestige among their peers and are elected to more school offices than early-maturing girls (Jones and Mussen, 1958). These findings are not clear-cut nor fully consistent, and substantial research must be done to clarify just what is going on. In addition, there has been no follow up of adult differences between early- and late-maturing girls, although the striptease study suggests that differences do persist.

We have now provided some detail on two of the three ways in which physique can effect socialization: through altering the probabilities that ego will enter one group or another; and through altering ego's form of interaction in a group. The third effect assumes that ego accepts his culture's ideas of "good" and "bad" physique and applies those evaluations to his own body, being proud if his physique is "good" and ashamed if it is "bad." For example, the United States of the 1970s has fairly specific notions of beauty. Women as well as men internalize these standards. Thus a girl with a large bust (relative to her waist) and small hips (relative to her bust) will evaluate herself as attractive, and as a result she will be more confident with men than her small-busted, large-hipped counterpart (other things being equal). The opposite was true in the 1920s and 1930s when smaller busts and relatively larger hips were the cultural vision of loveliness.[4] In the same vein, a man with a big penis may be more self-assured in his ro-

---

[4] The average bust-waist-hips dimensions of the 11 Miss Americas selected from 1921 to 1938 are 33-25-35. The averages for the 11 Miss Americas selected from 1960 to 1970 are 36-23-36. Earlier Miss Americas were generally shorter than recent ones, but the average difference is less than one inch (Long, 1969:462).

Figure 7–2.

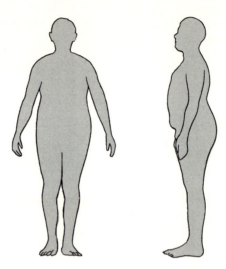

Predominant *endomorphy,* with minimal mesomorphy and with a slight secondary strength in ectomorphy. Somatotype: 7-1-1½. Regional somatotypes: 7-1-2, 7-1-1, 7-1-2, 7-1-2, 7-1-1.

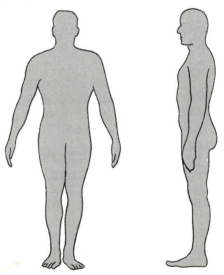

Predominant *mesomorphy,* with minimal endomorphy and with a slight secondary strength in ectomorphy. Somatotype: 1-7-1½. Regional somatotypes: 1-7-1, 1-7-2, 1-7-1, 1-7-2, 1-7-2.

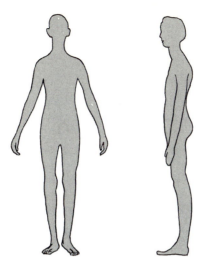

Predominant *ectomorphy*, with some slight secondary strength in both mesomorphy and endomorphy. Somatotype: 1½-1½-7. Regional somatotypes: 2-1-7, 1-2-7, 1-1-7, 2-2-6, 1-1-7.

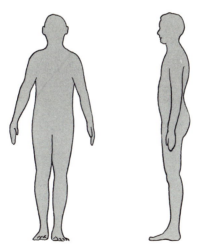

An *average* individual. This is a mid-range physique showing almost an even balancing among the three primary components. Somatotype: 4-3½-4. Regional somatotypes: 4-4-4, 4-3-3, 4-3-4, 4-4-4, 4-4-4.

mantic pursuits than his smaller counterpart (again, other things being equal) because the popular culture attributes enormous masculinity and virility to a large phallus (e.g., Puzo, 1969), in spite of the fact that size is not directly related to biological function. It is possible that the smaller man, suffering from doubts of his sexual adequacy, may in fact perform badly as a result of those doubts.[5]

These cultural evaluations and expectations for various physiques appear to explain the relationships between William Sheldon's famous (or infamous) "somatypes" and various behavioral characteristics. Sheldon (1940, 1942) analyzed body build in terms of three dimensions: *endomorphy* (roughly, the tendency to be pudgy), *mesomorphy* (tendency toward muscularity), and *ectomorphy* (the tendency to be skinny and bony). Some individuals represent pure somatypes, but most of us have components of all three types of build. Sheldon reported a close relationship between these physical dimensions and several temperamental characteristics, but apparently very few professional psychologists believed him. There were substantial methodological problems with his studies, mainly because he himself did both the somatype ratings and the temperamental ratings, so that they were highly subject to biasing effects. Several more objective studies have since verified many of the relationships, although they do appear to be somewhat weaker than originally reported (Child, 1950; Cortes and Gatti, 1965). Still, Sheldon's work has not been taken very seriously.[6]

Child's (1950) study gives a good picture of the personalities associated with the three somatypes. A large population of college men were somatyped and then given self-rating questionnaires. The behavioral items which best correlated with mesomorphy (muscularity) were: withstands pain easily; looks other people

---

[5] Male organs do indeed differ greatly in size when flaccid, but Masters and Johnson (1966) report that small penises expand more than large ones so that these differences become minimal during erection. Since the latter state is, after all, the relevant operational mode, perhaps wide dissemination of this information will lead to a shift in our national values.

[6] Gardner Lindzey points out that Sheldon's writings were "singularly adept at ridiculing or parodying just those aspects of the scientific posture of psychologists that are most sensitively, rigidly, and humorlessly maintained. One might argue convincingly that, if Sheldon had conducted the same research but had reported it in an appropriately dull, constricted, and affectless manner . . . , its impact upon the discipline might have been much greater" (1967:228).

right in the eye; desires strenuous physical exercise; likes cold showers; likes to swim nude; likes dangerous physical adventure. For brevity we may refer to these items as the "Tarzan syndrome." Fatter endomorphs and skinnier ectomorphs were not nearly as heroic. Endomorphs ate and slept well, were complacent, conforming, and amiable. Ectomorphs did not like pain, were not very sociable, did not like strenuous exercise, nude swimming, or dangerous adventures. A fascinating addition to this picture comes from several studies of criminal delinquency which report that delinquents are more likely to be mesomorphs than endo- or ectomorphs (Glueck and Glueck, 1956; Lindzey, 1967; Cortés and Gatti, 1970).

The correlations between somatype and personality may be explained by genetic and/or hormonal factors which affect both body and behavior. We are inclined, however, to accept a different explanation based on cultural expectations for various body types. In our culture, we expect a hero to be a mesomorph and a mesomorph to be a hero. If the society persists in attributing Tarzan-heroic qualities to the mesomorph, then the mesomorph will eventually attribute those qualities to himself, or at least he will answer a questionnaire as if he did. Several studies have investigated social stereotypes associated with the three somatypes, and indeed, most people evaluate a mesomorph in a positive, heroic manner (even though they know nothing about him other than his body build), while endo- and ectomorphs are evaluated negatively (Staffieri, 1967; Strongman and Hart, 1968; Lerner, 1969). If the cultural expectation explanation is correct, we would predict that tall, handsome mesomorphs will be more likely to have Tarzan syndrome than short, ugly mesomorphs. (Our assumption is that the culture has more heroic expectations for tall, handsome men than short, ugly ones.) Presumably we could improve on the physique-personality correlations which have been obtained to date if our measures of physique included height and handsomeness as well as somatype. If these inclusions did *not* improve the correlations, we would have to give more consideration to the possibility that genetic-hormonal factors jointly affect personality and physique.

Suggested Reading

The articles by E. Hess on "Imprinting" (*Science*, 130:133–141, 1959) and "Ethology" (in Brown, et al. (eds.), *New Directions in Psychology*. Holt, Rinehart and Winston, New York, 1962) are good overviews of work on imprinting.

Although one must be wary of the unqualified analogies among species, Konrad Lorenz *On Aggression* (Harcourt Brace Jovanovich, New York, 1966) offers numerous fascinating observations of social modification of innate behavioral traits in animals.

Gardner Lindzey presents a balanced discussion of the somatype controversy in his chapter "Behavior and morphological variation" (in J. Spuhler (ed.), *Genetic Diversity and Human Behavior,* Aldine Publishing Co., Chicago, 1967).

PART III

Biological Manipulation of Behavior

Until now we have confined ourselves to naturally occurring *biological factors. One major methodological strategy which can be used to show effects of biology on social behavior is the manipulation of biological factors purposively and observation of changes that result in social behavior. This is easier said than done. Often it is difficult to manipulate a specific biological factor without disturbing others, in which case isolation of the biological factor which made the difference is not achieved. This is further complicated by ethical constraints which prevent one from using a technique which has a potential for harm to the persons acting as subjects. Often we must rely on studies in which social behavior was changed as a result of biological manipulation thought to be therapeutic for persons who are ill, in which case the illness, previous therapy, or the persons' expectations may have produced the behavioral change observed. Where persons try to affect their own behavior biologically the factors which they wish to change or their expectations may result in behavior change. These problems will become more explicit as we examine some of the evidence on behavioral change resulting from biological manipulation.*

CHAPTER 8

BRAIN ALTERATION

ATTEMPTS TO MODIFY BEHAVIOR HAVE NOT been limited to socialization processes. To the degree that physiological factors have been thought to affect behavior, man has tried by various means to manipulate behavior by changing physiological mechanisms. In this chapter we will discuss some results of surgical and related mechanical techniques used to alter behavior such as various "shock therapies" and the implantation of electrodes in the brain. Chapter 9 will deal with pharmacologically evoked changes in behavior. We shall not discuss plastic surgery, prosthetic devices, and so on which may have an effect on behavior but which have not thus far been the object of much behavioral science research.

PSYCHOSURGERY

When extensive dissection of the anatomy pointed to the brain as the endpoint of nerve fibers, it was perhaps inevitable that man would try to alter behavior by brain surgery. Although they were based on somewhat less than scientific observations, early man had similar notions.

Surgery of the head is of comparatively recent origin but contains one operation which is probably the oldest in history. Trephining or 'trepanning,' the making of an opening in the skull, has been practised since the New Stone Age. These antique 'surgeons' used a flint scraper with which a circular portion of bone would be laboriously removed. Strangely enough some of their patients recovered, for skulls have been found which show the formation of new bone around the rim of the trephine hole, a clear proof of survival. The object of the operation was no doubt to allow escape of the imprisoned demon, who made his presence known by the convulsive movements of epilepsy or by intolerable headache (Cartwright, 1967).

We no longer accept the demon theory of aberrant behavior, but the development of techniques to change behavior without complete understanding of the "causes" of the behavior or all the possible consequences of the action taken has continued. Surgical separation of part of the frontal lobes from the remainder of the brain (lobotomy), as well as other techniques to be discussed, developed without such knowledge. On the basis of the successful treatment of experimentally induced "neurosis" in a chimpanzee by frontal lobotomy, similar operations were undertaken in man during the 1930s (Chatfield, 1953). An earlier similar operation performed in 1890 was not generally applied. From 1935 until the development of various drugs to treat the psychoses in the mid-1950s, thousands of mental patients had such surgery.

Although there is some evidence that relatively specialized functions are concentrated in various areas of the brain, exact knowledge of brain mechanisms, particularly the overall coordination and integration of motor, sensory, cognitive, speech functions, emotions, etc., is yet to be gained. Summarizing the implications of studies of electrical stimulation of various areas of the brain, one writer has noted that the interactions of various brain mechanisms are so complex that to speak of one small part having "a function" or as a "center" for some behavior is to oversimplify greatly (Jasper, 1961).

Surgical separation of parts of the frontal lobes does have some striking behavioral results. How much these results tell us about normal behavior in relation to brain structure is questionable because such operations have only been done on ill persons when many other forms of therapy have been tried and have failed. The unknown degree to which their diseases have altered normal functioning limits the degree to which one can generalize the findings to the nondiseased population.[1] And we do not know to what degree, if any, previous chemotherapy or shock therapy may have modified the functions of the disconnected tissue.

---

[1] To point this out, of course, is not to advocate that prefrontal lobotomies, or other procedures to be described here, should be done on persons who are not severely ill and for whom less radical modes of treatment are sufficient.

Lobotomies vary as to amount and location of tissue involved. The approximate location and relative degree of tissue in three types of lobotomy are illustrated in Figure 8–1. A number of studies of behavior of patients who had such lobotomies were done during the time that large numbers of patients had such surgery. Perhaps the best of these was done by an interdisciplinary team of investigators at what was then called the Boston Psychopathic Hospital (Greenblatt, 1953). Comparisons of patients before and after the operation on a number of psychological and social dimensions were done by physicians, psychologists, and sociologists.

After surgery, patients, most of whom suffered from some form of schizophrenia, were able to score higher on tests designed to measure ability to think abstractly in an organized fashion. Their associations were less "bizarre" and "incoherent"—that is, less evidently primary symptoms of schizophrenia—than before surgery (Levinson et al., 1953). Analysis of social interaction of the patients using standardized rating procedures indicated that they displayed greater tension-releasing behavior, joking, laughing, etc. Initiation of interaction with others in terms of offering opinions and expressing feelings was higher after surgery. However, asking for opinions from others and concern for others' feelings remained low, indicating a continuation of the lack of interest in others typical of schizophrenics. Significant decreases in display of tension, withdrawal, and antagonistic behavior were observed. Care of self as well as "total social adjustment" were judged to be improved in a significant number of patients (Barrabee, 1953).

Whether an outcome can be considered desirable or not is relative, depending on the social context to which the patient must return. For example, Greenblatt (1959) reports cases in which similar outcomes in terms of patient behavior produced quite different results in different contexts. In two female patients psychotic symptoms disappeared, but they were lacking in energy and initiative and no longer took an interest in cooking, housework, etc. One of them had a husband whom she had dominated before the surgery and who was quite happy with her changing disposition. In the second case, however, the husband was highly irritated at having to do the housework and became "disgruntled, thin, unhappy."

Some evidence for hemispheric dominance was found in the comparisons of unilateral lobotomy of the right and left sides. Generally, ability to abstract and organize thought was more improved by unilateral lobotomy of the patient's right hemisphere

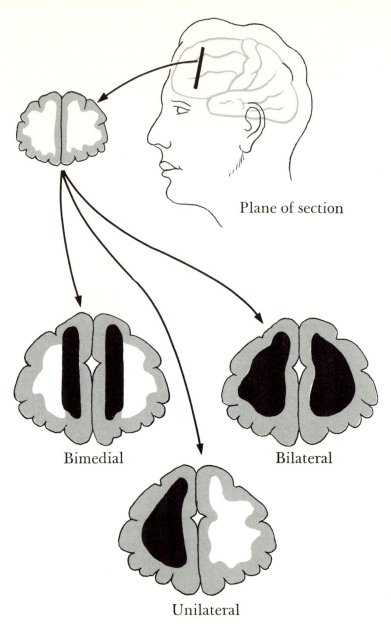

Plane of section

Bimedial

Bilateral

Unilateral

FIGURE 8–1. Diagrammatic illustration of the plan and extent of section of frontal tissue in the bimedial, bilateral, and unilateral lobotomies. Areas in which the tracts are severed are represented by parallel lines. (From *Frontal Lobes and Schizophrenia* by Milton Greenblatt and Harry C. Solomon, © 1953, Springer Publishing Company, Inc., N.Y.C.)

than by similar operations on the left (Greenblatt et al., 1953). However, the bimedial operation generally produced the above-mentioned psychological and social outcomes at a higher rate than the bilateral or unilateral surgery while it involved less tissue in the brain (Greenblatt and Solomon, 1953a). Effects also were more pronounced when emotional tension had been high preoperatively or the onset of illness had been more recent.

Lobotomies to reduce pain from terminal illness are effective in relieving some types of pain (Freeman and Watts, 1950) but attention spans and performance on various tests are usually lowered in patients who have had them (Greenblatt and Solomon, 1953). Again, one cannot be sure whether the illness itself or emotional reaction to either the illness or the operation produced the effect, rather than the surgery. Comparison with control groups who have had sham surgery, as is often performed on animals, is outside ethical bounds for human beings. If the effects are a consequence of the tissue separation, it is evident that the degree of "improvement" on social and psychological variables is relative, depending on the degree of preoperative deterioration and the nature of the illness.

While this discussion may seem academic given the decline in use of this type of surgery, there have been recent suggestions that lobotomy may have been too quickly abandoned and may be indicated when drug therapy fails (Brill, 1969). It appears that there is little to be gained in terms of more knowledge about behavior from these operations. The ethical dilemma of treating symptoms versus causes has been well summarized by Cobb:

In this field of cerebral psychophysiology it is obvious that the most up-to-date information must be used to relieve intractable pain and to show what parts of the brain can safely be injured in the removal of tumors and other lesions. The question of relieving mental suffering is more complex. The cause of the suffering may be largely psychological—for example, suffering due to social conflict. One may say, 'That makes no difference. Let us relieve this depressed mood by lobotomy, whatever its cause.' In the case of severe depression few physicians would object. Carrying this argument to its logical conclusions, however, would justify the lobotomizing of all unhappy persons—for example, all members of a depressed minority under a dictatorship. They would probably mostly become happier and more tractable. Once started on the practice of changing the moods and minds of people by surgery or chemistry, where does one stop? Social, legal, and moral implications need far more study before we take this road to 'peace of mind' (1961).[2]

[2] Reprinted with the permission of the University of Texas Press.

SHOCK THERAPY

Like lobotomy, the induction of convulsions or coma to treat psychoses by using various "shocking" agents began in the 1930s, bringing about similar problems regarding the obtaining of knowledge and the use of a technique without complete knowledge of its effects. The fact that "chains and flogging, ordeal by fire, drowning, suffocation and bleeding have been successfully used on psychotic individuals" (Freeman and Watts, 1950), prompted two writers to assure their audience that shock therapy did not grow out of such medieval tortures but developed "empirically" (Kalinowsky and Hoch, 1952). This is the polite way of saying that the therapist, no matter how humanistic his goal, tried a technique without a substantial theory as to its outcome or discovered something by accident.

Sakel (1938) discovered that mental patients who went into a coma when accidentally given large doses of insulin had reduced psychotic symptoms. This discovery led to the use of insulin-induced shock as a treatment of the psychoses. The "shock" or coma occurs because the insulin results in quick loss of the major energy source of the body, sugar. At about the same time as the discovery of insulin shock, on the assumption that schizophrenia and epilepsy rarely occurred together because of "a sort of biological antagonism," Meduna (1938) induced epilepticlike convulsions in schizophrenics by injecting cardiazol in the blood stream. He claimed "success" somewhat superior to insulin shock but estimated that either method accompanied by proper psychotherapy would be successful in over 50 percent of patients.

Based on similar assumptions, electrically induced shock was soon being used to produce convulsions. This treatment results in improvement in some schizophrenics, particularly when there are elements of depression present. Manic-depressive psychosis is even more responsive than schizophrenia to electroshock therapy in the depressive stage, with disappearance of the symptoms occurring in four out of five cases after about four treatments. However, permanent "cure" is usually not achieved (Kalinowsky and Hoch, 1952).

Although complications may occur from these treatments, such outcomes have become increasingly rare. If physicians using the treatments thoroughly examine patients beforehand and do not attempt treatment when it is known that the patient's condition increases the likelihood of some problem, complications are minimized. Patients do experience temporary amnesia after electroshock therapy but there is no evidence of permanent damage to the brain or other body systems when care is taken that complicating conditions are not present (Paterson, 1963). The lack of evidence does not mean, however, that such damage does not occur.

In spite of widespread usage and numerous studies, little more is known about why these treatments have the effect that they do than when the studies were first begun. From our discussion of neurohormone balance (in Chapter 6), it is obvious that a large dose of insulin results in multiple hormone and metabolic adjustments. Factors common to the shock therapies have been sought, and there are at least fifty hypotheses as to the possible common denominators (Kalinowsky and Hoch, 1952). Many body changes have been documented in some detail, but basic knowledge of how these changes affect psychoses, knowledge which might indicate which biological mechanisms effect mental states, is yet to be discovered.

Although these methods have been controversial because of their somewhat happenstance origin and their potential for misuse, such as for punitive rather than therapeutic purposes (Kesey, 1962), there is no question that through their use a lot of people have been saved from existing in a vegetative state in mental institutions (Paterson 1963). It is unfortunate that the effects of the shock therapies are so widespread in various body systems that knowledge of specific biological effects on behavior has not been forthcoming from study of their use.

ELECTRODES IN THE BRAIN

The more specific the knowledge of biological effects on behavior, the greater the possibility for control not only of disease but also control of behavior unrelated to disease. As is often the case, the techniques for gaining knowledge frequently are also useful for control of the phenomena being studied. Thus, the issues of what is defined as disease and who shall have the right to control a given person's behavior must continually be raised. The recent development of electrode implantation in the human brain, which can then be stimulated by remote-control devices, has brought us to the point that such considerations cannot be reserved for the future.

In contrast with lobotomy and shock therapy, electrode implantation in the brain was researched to a considerable degree in animals before it was attempted in human beings, and its application today in human beings is "relatively rare" (Schwitzgebel, 1968). Thus, just how much is to be learned from the use of this technique is an open question. The results thus far show considerable promise.

Olds (1960) was able to distinguish electrical stimulation of particular areas of the rat brain as "rewarding," "neutral," or "punishing." He devised an experiment whereby rats could electrically stimulate their own brains by pressing a pedal. Upon pressing the pedal, the rat received stimulation for one half-second, whereupon the stimulation ended and it was necessary to release and depress the pedal again for additional stimulation. By observing the frequency of pedal pressing, the degree of reward or punishment could be assessed, with frequent pressing indicating reward and complete avoidance indicating punishment.[3]

Placement of the electrodes was varied over numerous sites in the brain, and it was estimated that stimulation of 35 percent of the area of the rat brain was rewarding, 60 percent was neutral, and 5 percent was punishing. The behavior in response to rewarded areas was not unlike that of a child with respect to a cookie jar.

Sometimes, while the animal is self stimulating, the circuit is cut off by the experimenter. . . . An animal that is self stimulating gives a series of forceful ('frustrated' looking) responses and then turns away finally from the pedal to groom himself or sleep; but he will go back from time to time and press the pedal as though to make sure he's not missing anything (Olds, 1960).

Furthermore, Olds (1960) found evidence of relatively specific areas which mediate the primary drives of hunger and sex. In certain areas the amount of bar pressing by the rat was greater or less, depending on the length of time since the animal had been fed. Castrated animals, in which there is no androgen production, did not respond to stimulation of an area thought to have an effect on sex behavior. When androgen was injected into these animals, there was response to the electrical stimulation. Thus, it is possible to distinguish particular areas in the brain which are sensitive to hormonal and metabolic states of the body.

[3] Of course, there is an underlying assumption here that there is no such thing as a masochistic rat. Another interpretation of the result is that the rats were stimulating those sections of their brains which ensure the repetition of whatever motor act is otherwise being performed. If this were true, no "reward" would necessarily be involved.

However, the effects of stimulation also vary by intensity and duration of the stimulus relative to such behaviors as feeding, drinking, and gnawing (Mendelson, 1969). Through experiments controlling for their neural, hormonal, and behavioral effects, it may be possible to learn the specific mechanisms which regulate these and perhaps other drives.

To learn about these phenomena in man, however, is not so easily implemented as in the ingenious yet complicated experiments on animals. Electrodes have been implanted in men with interesting results but, again, interpretations of the results are complicated by the fact that such experiments are done only on patients who volunteer in the hope of gaining some therapeutic result. Not only may the disease process or the therapeutic regimen modify normal body functioning and make one's findings suspect (King, 1961), but some experiments, such as castration of such persons, are ethically out of the question.

However, studies of patients who have had electrodes placed in various regions of the brain reveal areas where the patients find the stimulation to be desirable and other areas in which stimulation is undesirable. These areas are similar to those which Olds found in animals (Heath, 1964).

Stimulation of a specific area does not control behavior in the sense that the person becomes a robot. Nevertheless, remarkable changes in mood and content of expressed thoughts occur with stimulation of particular areas. Patients were interviewed while they had electrodes placed in various areas of the brain and were stimulated at given points in the conversation without their knowing exactly when they were being stimulated. Their mood would change abruptly upon stimulation and they could not explain the reason for the change. Stimulation of the "pleasure areas" caused patients who were depressed and deprecating themselves to become optimistic and to discuss "pleasant experiences, past and anticipated" (Heath, 1964). Patients suffering with intractable pain from cancer gained "striking and immediate relief."

The aversive sites are described as follows (see Figure 8–2):

When the rostral hypothalamus was stimulated, patients complained of discomfort of the type usually associated with intense autonomic nervous system imbalance, i.e., abdominal discomfort, feelings of warmth, fullness in the head, and pounding heart. Application of stimuli to the midline tegmental region produced intense rage or fear or both, with impairment of ability to calculate and perform motor tests. . . . Extremely uncomfortable emotional reactions were induced

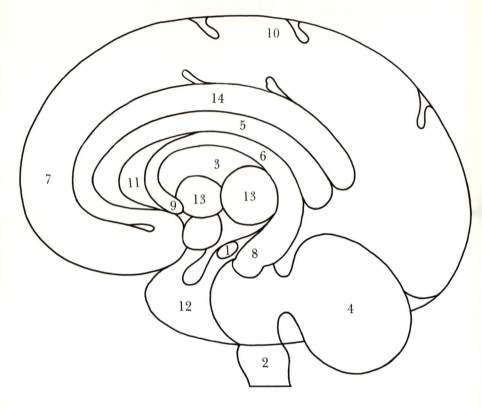

1. Amygdala
2. Brain stem
3. Caudate nucleus
4. Cerebellum
5. Corpus callosum
6. Fornix
7. Frontal lobe

8. Hippocampus
9. Hypothalamus
10. Motor cortex
11. Septal region
12. Temporal lobe
13. Thalamus
14. Transitional cortex

FIGURE 8-2. Diagram of the human brain. Adapted from J. M. R. Delgado, "ESB," *Psychology Today*, May 1970, p 49.

with stimulation . . . to the amygdaloid nucleus. Stimuli to the hippocampus were accompanied by pronounced anxiety, and one patient described a *déjà vu* phenomenon (Heath, 1964).

Although these results indicate a degree of specificity of effect, it should be noted that varying the level of current at a given site may change the effect (Bishop et al., 1964). Thus, it would be incorrect to assume that specific sites for specific feelings or behaviors have been isolated.

In addition to the above studies, Heath (1964) placed electrodes in patients who were subsequently allowed to control their own stimulation. An apparatus was developed which was portable (battery-powered) and which gave the patient a choice of three buttons to be pushed when stimulation was desired. One patient, suffering from narcolepsy (uncontrollable tendency to fall asleep), was able to control his condition to the degree that he could keep a job. He used the button connected to the septal area of the brain almost exclusively for this purpose. Observed pressing this button at a rapid rate on one occasion, he explained that the stimulation produced a feeling like sexual arousal. However, rapid sequential pressing of the button resulted in frustration and nervousness rather than orgasm.

A second patient proved to be particularly articulate in his description of subjective feelings when pressing buttons connected to electrodes in particular brain sites. This patient used one button an average of 488 times per hour. This button he thought was going to bring him a desirable and not simply pleasurable state—in this case recall of a memory—but which, when pushed, was frustrating because the state was not reached. He occasionally tried the "aversive sites" in spite of suffering discomfort from doing so. In contrast, the first patient placed a pin under one button which he disliked so that it could not be pushed.

BRAIN STIMULATION AND SOCIAL BEHAVIOR

Little systematic study of the effect of brain stimulation on social interaction has been done, but a few investigations among animals have illustrated the potential for this technique in interaction experiments. It is well known that, in a colony of monkeys, one monkey emerges as the "boss" and, therefore, has more territory relative to the other monkeys and has the choice of food and females. One such boss monkey with electrode implants was stimulated in the caudate nucleus for five seconds per minute over an hour's time. His gestures, postures, and facial expressions changed noticeably, and so did his social status. The other monkeys no longer stayed out of his territory or deferred to him in terms of other privileges. However, ten minutes after the stimulation was ceased, the boss monkey's dominance was reasserted. When a lever was placed on a wall inside the colony whereby the boss could be stimulated, a female monkey soon learned to pull the lever frequently and neutralize the dominance of the boss (Delgado, 1969a).

The sexual behavior of another pair of monkeys was strikingly effected by brain stimulation of the female. By remote control, a female was stimulated in the nucleus medialis dorsalis of the thalamus.

The animal moved its head backward and walked a few steps, avoiding the proximity of the other monkeys, jumped with precise coordination of movement to the back wall of the cage, where it hung for a few seconds, jumped down to the floor, and then walked back to the starting point, resuming the type of behavior which was interrupted by the stimulation. At the end of this sequence, if male monkey no. 4, which was the boss of the colony was present, he usually mounted monkey no. 10 (the stimulated female). This effect was so reliable that stimulations applied for 5 seconds once every minute during a 90 minute period produced a total of 81 mountings. No sexual relations were recorded before or after the stimulation period for the entire day (Delgado, 1964).

Aggression has also been evoked and provoked by brain stimulation. In studies of cats, Delgado (1964) found that stimulation of the lateral hypothalamus evoked aggression toward objects in the environment. The cats would attack another cat, a toy animal, or the experimenter. Stimulation of the anterior hypothalamus resulted in sham rage (hissing, arched back, bared teeth, etc.) without attack. However, when sham rage resulting from stimulation was displayed in the presence of an unstimulated cat, it was the latter cat who attacked the one showing sham rage. Aggression can be evoked by stimulation in monkeys, but the target for aggression varies according to social status within a colony. The artificially aggressive monkey attacks those lower than himself in the social hierarchy but not the boss monkey or others of higher rank. If he is of the lowest rank, overt aggression does not occur (Delgado, 1969a).

One can easily see how stimulation techniques could be used

in systematic experiments to delineate the relative effects of sex, aggression, rank, etc., on interindividual relationships, the overall state of group relationships, and so on. By being able to control these factors in any or all group members, it is possible to do controlled experiments where it was only possible to develop statistical correlations in the past.

Such experiments are not likely to be done on men, at least on "normal" men, for ethical reasons. Nevertheless, it may be possible to learn a great deal about these behaviors when such techniques are used for therapeutic purposes. Presently a group of physicians is using stimulation techniques and surgery in an attempt to control unprovoked violent attack in selected patients. One such patient had plunged a knife into the heart of a stranger in a washroom and, subsequently, attacked a nurse with a pair of scissors, stabbing her in the lung (Mark et al., 1969). Through an electrode implant in the amygdala it was possible to provoke similar attack behavior by stimulation. A lesion was then made at the site of the stimulation in the hope that the mechanism of the behavior could be interrupted. Judgment of success must await long-term follow up of this and other patients and comparison with similarly selected control groups who did not receive stimulation or lesions.

CONCLUSIONS

Whether or not use of the procedures just discussed, if continued, will reveal much more about the functions of the brain relative to behavior than is now known is problematic. Stimulation of an area by an electric current is not the same as the normal stimulation or, perhaps more accurately, the interchange of stimuli among various elements of the brain. If electrodes can be developed as unobtrusive monitoring devices so that the normal interstimulation of particular brain elements can be measured without the electrode implant itself modifying them, knowledge can be gained by correlating these measurements with those of other body states, such as hormone levels, and with measures of emotional and social behavior. Such procedures may soon be possible with the increased miniaturization of electronic devices and some such experiments are being done with animals.[4] We

[4] Various such monitoring devices are used to measure certain body states of astronauts and cosmonauts. However, to our knowledge, none of these men has had such devices placed in the brain.

suspect that more knowledge of normal behavior will be gained by monitoring devices than by stimulating devices, although the latter may be useful for performing experiments as noted above once the degree to which they simulate "natural" stimuli is determined.

Whether human beings, diseased or not, should be asked to volunteer for studies using such devices is a difficult ethical question. There is some risk in even the best tested surgical procedure. And, although the potential volunteer may be made fully aware of the risk, some would question whether the experimenter has the right to ask him to participate or, indeed, whether he has the right to volunteer himself. Even in the case that some therapy may result, some researchers have argued that chemotherapy is preferable to such devices as brain stimulators (Heath, 1964). This may be true in terms of the practicality of use in large populations, but it may be possible to effect a more localized and specific change with a few electrodes than with a drug or shock which is disseminated throughout the body with possible unknown effects on various systems.

Two recent reviews of the use of electromechanical devices to modify behavior (Delgado, 1969b; Schwitzgebel, 1968) take quite different positions on the possibilities of misuse of such devices. Both discussed the potential for remote control of various mechanisms to monitor and stimulate behavior by a combination of implanted electrodes linked through miniaturized transmitters to some central control source such as a computer. Delgado (1969b) writes:

Fears have been expressed that this new technology brings with it the threat of possible unwanted and unethical remote control of the cerebral activities of man by other men, but this danger is quite improbable and is outweighed by the expected clinical and scientific usefulness of the method.

Schwitzgebel (1968), on the other hand, warns that gadgetry is sometimes used simply because it is available and that mechanistic, impersonal "solution" of problems which involve complex personal and interpersonal factors may not really be a solution at all. That agreement on what behavior should be controlled and by whom has not been reached is well illustrated in current controversies over, for example, the use of birth control devices or psychedelic drugs.

Knowledge of how to evoke painful and pleasurable stimuli, and aggressive and other behaviors, as well as the means of monitoring behavior, both by remote control, does not allow for complete control over behavior, but the potential even for considerable control is startling. The degree of skill and the technology involved will no doubt limit the number of persons who use such devices and the degree of their use. However, since knowledge is not exclusively found among the wise and scrupulous,[5] such devices will sooner or later be misused.

Suggested Reading

An interdisciplinary team reports the most comprehensive study of frontal lobotomy in Milton Greenblatt and Harry C. Solomon (eds.), *Frontal Lobes and Schizophrenia* (Springer Publishing Co., New York, 1953).

Some known results and implications of electrode implantation and stimulation of animal and human brains are presented by José M. R. Delgado, a leading practitioner of the method, in his *Physical Control of the Mind* (Harper & Row, New York, 1969).

The general issues involved in physical modification of behavior are explored in Perry London, *Behavior Control* (Harper & Row, New York, 1969).

---

[5] The best evidence of this is found in an account of the "experiments" carried out by prominent physicians and scientists in Nazi Germany. See Mitscherlich and Mielke (1949).

CHAPTER 9

DRUGS

NUMEROUS SUBSTANCES, INJECTED, IN-
gested, inhaled, or otherwise introduced into the human body,
have an effect on behavior. These substances are a subset of a
larger set of substances called drugs, many of which have no
behavioral consequences. We shall not get into the problem of
defining the term "drug" nor shall we survey every drug known
to have some effect, direct or indirect, on behavior. The discussion of a few issues involving relatively commonly used drugs
should serve to illustrate the complex interaction of psychophysiological states, drugs, and social behavior.

The assessment of drug effect involves a number of variables:
physical, social, and psychological state of the organism before
intake; identification of the expected effect (which is apparently
important in placebo effect and addiction); tolerance to the drug
over time; presence or absence of withdrawal symptoms when the
drug is no longer used (also important in addiction); effect on
specific cellular and physiological mechanisms; and method of
intake. Studies often deal with only one or two of these factors,
and, since they are often interrelated, complete understanding of
the effects of any given drug is yet to be obtained. Part of the
problem, of course, is that the complexity of the functioning
organism without the added effects of drugs is not completely
understood.

Dubos (1964) has noted the lack of a theory in the development and testing of drugs. Like the procedures discussed in the
preceding chapter, most drugs were discovered "empirically,"
their eventual use being quite different from that originally
intended. Others were discovered by accident or were used long

before they were investigated scientifically. Alcohol is discussed in the Bible, and Shen-Nung, a Chinese scholar-emperor, described cannibis (marijuana) about 2737 B.C. (Bloomquist, 1968). The psychophysiological effects of LSD were first experienced by a Swiss chemist who accidentally ingested it while working on ergot-related compounds for quite another purpose (Geller and Boas, 1969). Iproniazid, now used for its euphoric effect on some depressed mental patients, was first thought to be a treatment for tuberculosis (Barber, 1967). Thus the terms "main effect" and "side effects" are used, depending on the purpose of the prescriber or user, while the actual total effects of any given drug are not entirely known. As Titmuss (1964:244) notes, this is not a new situation: "Two hundred years ago Voltaire defined medical treatment as the art of pouring drugs of which one knew nothing into a patient of whom one knew less."

PLACEBO EFFECT

Perhaps the most difficult task in assessing the psychological and behavioral effects of drugs is to distinguish the effect of the drug from the effect of belief in the drug or social setting in which the drug is taken. The latter are called placebo effects. Persons often report changes in psychological state or behave differently when they think they have taken a drug which they actually have not taken. When drugs thought to have psychological or behavioral effects are studied, it is (or should be) standard practice to give the drug to a random set of persons and give a separate but comparable group a placebo, such as a saline or lactose solution, which they think is the drug. To prevent the effect of experimenter expectations, which may be quite subtle, the experimenter should not know who has been given the drug or the placebo until the experiment is completed. This is usually called the "double blind" design.

The proportion of people who report relief of pain or other effects when given placebos is remarkable. Beecher (1964) reported the following range of percentages of persons reporting a change of psychological or physical states in a summary of numerous studies of persons receiving placebos: pain from a severe postoperative wound: 21–53%; cough: 36–43%; mood change: 30%; pain of angina pectoris: 26–38%; headache: 52%; seasickness: 58%; anxiety and tension: 30%; common cold: 35%. It appears that an average of 35 percent of people claim some effect of a drug which they think they have received when, in fact, they have received a nonactive substitute. In viewing studies of drug effects without controls for placebo effect or upon hearing subjective reports of drug effects, one should be aware that factors other than the drug itself may have produced the outcome.

Because of the possibility of placebo effect or the effects of previous psychological state, physical state, or social environment, the classification of drugs according to behavioral effects is precarious. For any given drug, a physician, acquaintance, or user knows of the exceptional case—one who acted contrary to expectation.

ADDICTION AND DEPENDENCE

Probably the most controversial classification system for drugs is specification of the degree to which they are addictive or the degree to which persons are "psychologically dependent" on drugs. There are few arguments that there are people addicted to opium derivatives (morphine, heroin, etc.) and alcohol. However, the lines between the nonaddicted heavy drinker and the alcoholic are vague. Some researchers argue that anyone who uses opium derivatives for relatively short periods of time will become an addict; others claim that there are occasional users who do not become addicted and that addiction occurs as a result of identification of the drug with physical withdrawal symptoms (Lindesmith, 1968). Both schools of thought tend to agree that addiction is more likely the greater the severity of physical withdrawal symptoms. These symptoms occur only after prolonged heavy use in the case of alcohol, whereas only relatively short-term use of opium derivatives will produce severe withdrawal symptoms when use is discontinued.

Even after physical withdrawal symptoms have ceased, the person who has been addicted usually craves the opiates or alcohol. Whether or not this craving has a physiological base or is different in kind from the craving found in those who use drugs which produce no physical withdrawal symptoms is unknown. Instead of drawing a line between addiction and psychological dependence, it might be more accurate to say that alcohol and opiates in doses sufficient to produce physical withdrawal are addictive *and* produce psychological dependence. Psychological dependence in this context is the craving of the drug in the belief that it is needed for adequate functioning.

The use of any drug may result in psychological dependence for some people. The person who must have caffeine, nicotine, or an amphetamine to get through the day, a few drinks to get through the evening, or sleeping pills to get through the night is as psychologically dependent on the drug being used as is the person who must have marijuana or LSD to have a "religious experience" or to be "creative."

PSYCHOSOCIAL CORRELATES OF DRUG USE

The psychological testing of drug users has been widespread and rather unremarkable in its results. For example, Lisansky (1967) reviewed numerous studies of projective tests, personality inventories, and IQ tests of alcoholics and concluded that one learns little of the etiology of alcoholism from such studies. We must rely on subjective reports of users and nonusers and historical accounts (each of which has poor reliability and validity) for hypotheses as to the psychosocial etiology of drug use.

The term "drug culture" has been used recently to refer to a segment of young people who have begun using various "mind altering" drugs. It is more accurate to refer to many drug cultures for there have been normative standards for drug use by subsets of populations in virtually all known societies. Rules for drug use have been based on age, sex, race, religious status—the usual factors on which social norms are based. For example, marijuana is used for religious purposes in segments of societies in Asia where alcohol is illegal, and alcohol is used in ceremonies of some religions in the United States where the possession of marijuana is illegal. The historical origins of such practices are often obscure, but it is clear that social groups have seen fit to regulate the use of drugs and designate who shall and who shall not be users.[1] As with other behaviors, the regulation is sometimes by legal means and sometimes through the use of nonlegal sanctions.

The groups which use drugs illegally or in the face of moral sanctions are referred to as "deviant subcultures" by students of deviancy. The degree to which the sanctions are enforced, the method of punishment, and, in the case of alcohol and the opiates, the addictive state and the cost of maintaining the "habit," all contribute to the formation of subgroups which develop their

---

[1] The history of the legal statuses of some drugs in the United States has been well documented and is worth reading. See, for example, Solomon (1966), Bloomquist (1968), Lindesmith (1968), Blum et al. (1969).

own rules regarding use of the drug, systems for obtaining the drug, and so on.

Perhaps the phenomenon most common to all drug use, legal or illegal, is that few people decide completely on their own to begin using a given drug. There is a process of interpersonal influence whereby nonusers are initiated to use of the drug. Chein et al. (1964), studied 500 cases of drug use which had come to the attention of courts or hospitals in New York from 1949 to 1952. Seventy-five percent of the users reported that they had been introduced to the drug by a peer or a group of peers, and an additional 15 percent had been introduced to it by an adult or a relative. Only 10 percent obtained the drug entirely of their own volition. Also significant is the fact that one-third of the users did not know what drug they had been given.

Although these self-reports are subject to question as to their accuracy, descriptions of initial drug use by sociologists who have spent some time in one or another group with a "drug culture" tend to confirm these observations. That which is illegal or banned by one's family, religious, or other group presents a challenge to the more adventurous. Others desire the respect of a user and, when asked to "get high" or to "turn on," they are unlikely to refuse. The process may not be too different from the acceptance of a cup of coffee to avoid offending a hostess or acceptance of a cigarette by a girl on a date to show her "sophistication."

Although for a time in some groups there has been a tendency to use whatever drug happened to be available, generally there are norms in even the most nonconforming of groups with respect to conditions under which drugs are used, the type of drugs considered as proper and improper, and age and other criteria for who shall be eligible for drug use. For example, in the San Francisco Bay area during its pinnacle as *the* drug scene in the United States, the "speed freak" (one who shoots amphetamines into the veins) came to be disdained and considered deviate by other drug users (Carey and Mandel, 1968).

For some drugs, the initial use requires some guidance, and the nature of this guidance may have a profound effect on the experience itself as well as on subsequent use of the drug. Initial use of marijuana requires not only proper instruction as to how to inhale the smoke but also identification by others as to when the smoker is "high." If the marijuana is improperly smoked, the effect on the nervous and other systems will not occur and the individual may merely experience choking, coughing, etc., particularly if he is unused to smoking. If he is smoking properly, he may claim no alteration in sensation, etc., but those around him may tell him he is "high" because of the content of his utterances, giggling, dilated pupils, or other indications that the drug is having some effect (Becker, 1953).

Initial ingestion of the much more powerful LSD requires no guidance (it is usually swallowed in a sugar cube), but lack of guidance through the experience while under the drug's influence can be disastrous. Users may perceive problems or memories which were previously subconscious, may think they are losing part of their bodies, may experience extreme depression, or may fear the loss of sanity, any of which perceptions may result in behavior dangerous to the individual and those around him. However, the individual using LSD is described as "hypersuggestible" and, if he has a sympathetic and knowledgeable guide, may be led from the above perceptions to opposite extremes of euphoria (Cohen, 1968).

Becker (1967) suggests that occasionally reported cases of "drug psychosis," particularly associated with the hallucinogens (LSD, marijuana, psilocybin, peyote) and sometimes with other drugs, could be a result of the severe anxiety reaction which may occur with severe perceptual distortion. If the person is taken to a hospital and confined, the notion that he is "losing his mind" may be reinforced, particularly if his behavior is labeled as psychotic. This argument assumes that severe anxiety reaction coupled with perceptual distortion and other drug effects simulates psychosis sufficiently to result in such a diagnosis.

This may be so, but a chemical powerful enough to affect perceptual and behavioral mechanisms to the degree that LSD apparently does no doubt interacts with the basic elements of the nervous system. Since we do not know the basic biochemical changes which occur in non-drug-induced psychosis, it is not possible to say that the hallucinogens produce the same results. There is evidence that persons with so-called "psychological problems" before taking these drugs may be particularly susceptible to severe reaction to the drug, as noted in the following sections on particular drugs.

BEHAVIORAL EFFECTS OF SELECTED DRUGS

At the risk of being repetitious, we must emphasize that there are exceptions to any generalizations about the effects of drugs. There are too many factors which effect the initial use of drugs, their continued use, and the outcome of such use to make unequivocal statements about behavioral or other consequences. It is possible to state some probable effects of drugs on behavior with these qualifications in mind. Here we can treat briefly only a few selected examples. From the early 1950s to 1967, over 12,000 patents were filed for drugs believed to have some psychological or behavioral effect (Geller and Boas, 1969). Even the drugs known before that time have not been properly studied, and we must confine ourselves to those few about which something is known and which are used in sufficient volume to be important.

Alcohol

Users of alcohol report varied effects: "It relaxes me," "It's a pick-me-up," "It really doesn't affect me; I just drink to be sociable." Carefully designed studies of the effects of alcohol do not support many of these assertions.

In one such study by Nash (1962), subjects were given a pungent, grape-colored drink without knowing the contents. One group received the ethyl alcohol equivalent of four martinis, a second group was given the equivalent of two martinis, a third group received the caffeine equivalent of three cups of coffee, and a final group was given a placebo. Each subject had not eaten for several hours, and all subjects were given a series of tests and a second maintenance dose after two hours.

After sufficient time for the drugs to take effect, there were practically no differences in self-ratings of relaxation, irritability, self-satisfaction, physical discomfort, tiredness, capability of close attention, impulsiveness, being "keen and alive," interest in the tests, or dislike of a puncture for a blood sample. The heavy alcohol group did show reduced confidence in their judgment.

On various tests of intellectual efficiency, the heavy alcohol group did significantly worse and the caffeine group did somewhat better than the light alcohol and placebo groups. Heavy alcohol produced particularly marked impairment on tests requiring vision, but the persons in this group also did poorly on verbal tests of digit memory, which indicates that more than visual impairment was involved. Although there were no significant differences among the groups on tests of abstract reasoning, the heavy alcohol group were "markedly impaired" in "the anticipation of needs arising in novel situations" and other measures of critical judgment.

These findings agree with what is known about the physical effects of alcohol. It has been described as a "depressant" or "anesthetic" in its effect on the nervous system (Kendis, 1967). St. Laurent and Olds (1967) have observed the self-stimulating behavior of rats given alcohol with electrodes implanted in various areas of the brain and have concluded that most of the posterior "deeper" areas of the brain are unaffected by alcohol, but the anterior areas which receive most environmental messages are greatly affected. It appears that alcohol primarily modifies the stimuli which are input from the environment. Others have speculated that the depression of central nervous system activity by alcohol results in the dominance of emotional impulses (Forney, 1967). According to this viewpoint, either the underlying emotional state of the individual or the emotions being expressed by others in the environment will be manifested and perhaps magnified by the effects of alcohol on the nervous system.

Heavy drinking is associated with various social problems. Marital difficulties, indebtedness, arrest for nonalcohol-related offenses, and numerous other problems are found among persons who have been arrested for driving under the influence of alcohol (cf. Waller, 1967). Persons involved in arguments or altercations with their assailants prior to homicide are likely to have alcohol in the blood at autopsy (Baker et al., 1971). Whether use of alcohol and its behavioral consequences are the primary reasons for these problems or whether these problems and drinking are the consequences of other factors is not known. Given the effects of alcohol on the nervous system and the addiction of a subset of drinkers, it is likely that alcohol usage is more than a peripheral factor.

One of the most consistent correlates of heavy alcohol use, documented in a number of studies (Haddon and Bradess, 1959; McCarroll and Haddon, 1962; Birrell, 1965; Neilson, 1965; Baker et al., 1971) is the incidence of deaths in or by automobiles. In single-car crashes, pedestrian deaths, and multiple-car crashes in which a given driver is at fault, the drivers' or dead pedestrians' blood alcohol concentrations far exceed those in the blood of comparable persons at the same site at a comparable time of day and year. It is estimated that over 50 percent of the more than 50,000 deaths per year in automobile-related incidents in the United States involve persons who have consumed extraordinary amounts of alcohol (Haddon et al., 1968). Sometimes other factors such as a faulty automobile or poor road conditions are also factors in these deaths. However, the performances of intoxicated

drivers in driving simulators reveal multiple errors in accelera-
tion, braking, signaling, and speed when compared with those
of nonintoxicated drivers in the simulator (Crancer et al.,
1969), which leads one to the conclusion that the visual and critical
judgment effects of excessive drinking are among the primary
factors in the alcohol-related deaths.

Opiates

Perhaps surprising to many is the fact that use of the opiates
(heroin, morphine, codeine) does not create euphoria, or a "good
feeling," in all who take them. Many persons experience severe
nausea and vomiting upon initial use (Chein et al., 1964). The
key to the intense craving for the drug by addicts and many who
have managed to withstand the pains of withdrawal is apparently
the effectiveness of the drug in relieving other pains. Detachment
from pain and anxiety is the reason most often given by addicts
when they return to use of the drug after withdrawal.

Opiate addiction was, until recently, mostly confined to the
most economically deprived areas of cities (Chein et al., 1964)
where, presumably, the drug provides insulation from the pains
of poverty and disease. Exceptions to this pattern were members
of the medical profession whose having prescribed morphine for
themselves or members of their families during a period of pain
or stress resulted in addiction (Pescor, 1966). More recently,
opiates have been used by some hippie and related groups from
the middle class, and among soldiers in Vietnam.

Opiate addicts have been labeled as neurotic or psychopathic,
or as having abnormal personalities. Since these labels often are
given automatically to someone who is addicted to drugs, it is not
possible to say whether particular personality types are more
likely to become addicted, whether addicts are likely to develop
changes in personality, whether the personality characteristics
are a function of other factors which also lead to addiction, or
whether the labels themselves are invalid (Isbell, 1966). Laboratory experiments to investigate these possibilities concerning
opiates in man are impossible because of the high risk of addiction. Some authors argue that animal experiments are insufficient
because addiction involves the labeling of the withdrawal
symptoms as associated with the drug. Animals without a language system, it is claimed, do not become addicted (Lindesmith,
1968).

However, addiction which amazingly parallels that in man

has been shown in animal experiments. Weeks (1964) placed rats in a box with a pedal which, when pressed, triggered the release of measured amounts of morphine into the blood stream through an attachment which allowed the animal to move about freely. The drug was first injected once per hour by the experimenter for 122 hours to create dependence whereupon the injections by the experimenter ceased. The rats quickly learned to get morphine by pressing the pedal and pressed it every two hours on the average. When the dosage per pedal press was reduced, the rats increased the number of presses to maintain the "habit."

Completely stopping the morphine injections resulted in symptoms similar to those in human addicts during withdrawal. The rats "became nervous and agitated (but never vicious), breathed rapidly, tried to escape from their cages and were sensitive to handling as if being touched were painful. Gastrointestinal activity increased, the feces became soft, and by the next morning the rats had suffered as much as a 20 percent loss in weight. They were sick rats, but a single injection put an end to their symptoms" (Weeks, 1964:48). The rats differed from human addicts in one respect; they did not anticipate their need by pressing the pedal ahead of time.

These results suggest that opiate addiction is primarily the result of use of the drug to avoid pain. An animal capable of learning is capable of associating pain relief with obtaining the drug. Once the drug is used, avoidance of withdrawal pain is the primary reason for use. No experiments are known in which animals learn to avoid other types of pain by drug use, but it should be possible to design such an experiment to test the hypothesis that animals can become addicted in this fashion.

The anticipation of withdrawal symptoms in human addicts results in intense activity, depletion of financial resources, and, frequently, criminal behavior to gain money to buy the drug. Other behavioral effects include drowsiness and inhibited hunger and sex drives (Isbell, 1966). The effects of opiates on driving and other behaviors have not been as well researched as the effects of alcohol. One study of 6,000 addicts registered with the Narcotic Addiction Control Commission in New York found that only 20 percent had a driver's license or a driving record. However, within this group, 75 percent had at least one accident or a conviction for violation of a traffic law unrelated to drugs as compared with about 20 percent of all New York drivers who have had accidents or convictions. Again, it is not known to what degree the drug per se contributed to this difference (Babst et al., 1969).

Cannabis

There are two varieties of the hemp plant, *Cannabis sativa*. The type which grows in the western hemisphere is the milder of the two and is commonly known as *marijuana*. The eastern hemisphere type is considerably more potent and is called *hashish*. The flowering top or leaves when smoked or otherwise consumed produce what is called a "high." There is, apparently, a particular substance, tetrahydrocannabinol (THC), which produces such an effect on the nervous system (Mechoulam et al., 1970). Presumably, although dose response curves have not been developed, the degree of THC which reaches the nervous system determines the degree of effect. The amount in the plant from which the cigarette is made, and the way in which it is smoked, are both important in the degree of effect.

In the mid-1930s there was a marijuana scare in the United States during which opponents attributed a variety of crimes and other social ills to marijuana usage. As a result, in 1937 Congress legislated the Marijuana Tax Act which, in effect, made the possession of marijuana illegal (Solomon, 1966). As a further result, use of marijuana for research purposes became very difficult and, with the exception of studies commissioned in 1938 by Mayor La Guardia of New York, little research on the effects of marijuana was done until the recent upsurge in use primarily among the young. At this writing, our knowledge of the drug's effects is not much advanced over the 1938 studies (Hollister, 1971).

The Mayor's Committee on Marijuana concluded that aggression, criminal behavior, unusual sexual behavior, and similar effects which had been attributed to the drug by opponents could not be found. In 1938 marijuana was used mainly by persons in minority groups who were without jobs and who were seeking distraction from boredom. Since the 1960s the population of users is clearly broader than that, although the full extent of marijuana use is not known. In the 1930s smoking usually occurred in small groups where the atmosphere was "friendly and sociable," and the same appears to be true today.

Hollister cites a number of effects of marijuana use from a recent clinical study: "On self-reporting mood scales, our subjects became more friendly initially, but less so with the passage of time; less aggressive, especially late in the course; less clear-thinking persistently; sleepy, especially after 3 hours; euphoric persistently;

and dizzy persistently" (Hollister, 1971:23). Physical effects include increased pulse rate and blood pressure.

Psychotic states of delirium or extreme anxiety were found in a minority of users, but there was also evidence of psychosis, drug addiction, epilepsy, or other problems prior to using marijuana. There was some impairment of coordination and motor functions, particularly involving more complex tasks. Time sense was altered, hearing less discriminant, and vision apparently sharper although there were visual distortions. On some intellectual tasks performance accuracy was maintained while speed was reduced, and on others speed was maintained while accuracy was impaired. All these effects were temporary, however, and there was no evidence that the drug was addictive. On the other hand, there was no evidence of the improved thinking or creative ability which some proponents have claimed (Wallace et al., 1966).

Given the detachment and motor effects of marijuana, one suspects that activities requiring concentration and coordination, such as driving, would be dangerous while a person was under the influence of the drug. Users have reported close calls resulting from such interest in a light or sound that it caused them to take their hands from the wheel (Bloomquist, 1968). In the driving simulator, marijuana effects are not nearly as severe as alcohol effects, but there is evidence that speedometer-monitoring errors occur more frequently when the driver is using marijuana (Crancer et al., 1969). Hollister (1971) asked his subjects, when they were "high," if they felt they could drive a car then. Without exception the answer was negative. A study of the driving records of 79 persons arrested for marijuana use revealed a greater number of violations for reckless driving, hit and run, and negligent driving, as well as a higher accident rate when compared with that of the total population of the county in which they were arrested (Crancer and Quiring, 1968). Whether these records were caused by marijuana use or by other factors concomitant with marijuana use is not known.

LSD

There is some similarity between the effects of marijuana and LSD, but the LSD effects are much more extreme and more numerous. Vision is blurred; nausea, dizziness, feeling of weakness, and tremors often occur. Perception of shape and color is altered, and the senses seem to overlap, e.g., music is described as being seen as well as heard. Mood changes are frequent and occur in a roller coaster fashion. The user often feels detached from other people and has an altered image of self, others, and his environment, which is described sometimes as beautiful and other times as horrible (Hollister, 1968). Not all who take LSD experience these effects. Changes are not reported by about 10 percent of persons who have had a "standard" dose (100μg). There is apparently some degree of "fighting off" the effects of ordinary doses. And, as we have noted, the person who has taken the drug is usually subject to guidance regarding what he will experience (Cohen, 1968).

The effects of LSD on intellectual functions appear to be profound, but it is difficult to distinguish them from perceptual distortions of the inputs of various tests. Memory, ability for problem solving, perception of relationships among objects, attention, and concentration are all temporarily impaired by LSD. The improved artistic creativity which is claimed by some users is not confirmed by objective judges of those users' creative efforts (Hollister, 1968). Users have also claimed better job performance and more love for others as effects of LSD, but coworkers report a deterioration in performance, and love is apparently expressed for mankind in general rather than for individuals since difficulties in close relationships with others sometimes result (Fisher, 1968).

The evaluation of these reported findings is confounded by the fact that persons with various problems may be more predisposed toward taking the drug as an escape from or in search of a solution to their problems. Illicit LSD users, when compared with nonusers matched for age, sex, and social class, tend to be "underachievers," and many have histories of psychosis or "conduct disorders." Almost all the users in one study had personality profiles (as measured by a standardized test) which were different from those of most persons who have taken the tests. Evidence indicated, however, that most of these differences were present before the users began taking the drug (Smart and Fejer, 1969).

Amphetamines

The amphetamines are produced in numerous forms as "pep pills," "diet pills," etc. In some cases they are prescribed by physicians for narcolepsy or obesity and, paradoxically, for calming hyperactive children. More often, they are obtained without prescription and are taken to keep awake while driving, working, or studying long hours. In larger doses, they are used by the "speed freak" who injects them into his veins.

The exact mechanisms involved in amphetamine action are

unknown, but amphetamines are similar to adrenalines in their chemical structure and physiological effects. Increased heart rate and blood pressure, dilated pupils, constriction of blood vessels, elevated muscle tension, and increased blood sugar occur in most adults when they take amphetamines (Ban, 1969).

Critics of the widespread use of amphetamines note that their effects are much stronger than the adrenalines' and that more appropriate drugs are now available for narcolepsy, obesity, and other conditions for which amphetamines are used. They point to the danger of psychological dependence and such other effects as "nervousness, insomnia, headache, irritability, and excessively increased motor activity," as contraindications to their use (Clement et al., 1970).

Tolerance to these drugs increases, and an unknown number of people have taken increased dosages which have resulted in malnutrition and hallucinations. A study of patients at the Public Health Service Narcotic Hospital in Lexington, Kentucky, who, when they entered, were taking more than 30 milligrams of amphetamines per day, revealed a pattern of psychosis. Reports of visual hallucinations, hearing voices, and paranoid reactions were common. Since many of these persons had histories of conflict with authority, social withdrawal, or psychiatric hospitalizations unrelated to drug use, it was not possible to determine the degree to which their symptoms were the result of drugs, were exacerbated by drugs, or were independent of drug use (Ellinwood, 1967).

In addition to hallucinations and paranoid delusions, those who inject amphetamines into their veins display fixations such as working on mechanical objects for hours but making no headway in terms of the functioning of the object. The lack of accomplishment from these prolonged efforts, however, does not seem to disturb them. They are similarly oblivious to hunger and the need to sleep. A typical week for the intravenous user consists of three to six days of injecting the drug every two hours, followed by 12 to 18 hours of sleep. The user often does not sleep or eat for days, but some users eat in spite of the lack of hunger and induce sleep with the help of barbiturates or heroin. Many have a history of heroin addiction. Although there is a "withdrawal syndrome" which includes prolonged sleep and lethargy, the excruciatingly painful symptoms of opiate withdrawal are not present when the intravenous amphetamine user quits the drug (Kramer et al., 1967). Thus, one may argue that addiction does not occur, but, as Clement et al. (1970) point out, the continued use and debilitating consequences of amphetamines taken intravenously are sufficiently severe that the matter of addiction is immaterial.

Sedatives and Hypnotics

Many drugs are widely used to induce sleep or relieve acute anxiety. The effects of these drugs vary somewhat according to chemical structure (barbiturates, bromides, chloral hydrate, paraldehyde) and dosage as well as characteristics of the patient or other user, particularly age. Some also act as anticonvulsants. Whereas most adults respond with reduced motor activity, drowsiness, and, after larger doses, deep sleep [2] (Thompson and Schuster, 1968), children and some elderly adults become irritable and are unable to sleep when given these drugs. Delirium rather than sedation is found in some patients with diagnosed psychopathology when given barbiturates (Ban, 1969).

Repeated use of even low doses of barbiturates often results in psychological dependency to "relieve anxiety" or to "go to sleep." Because of increased tolerance to the drug, larger doses are taken, and toxic effects are not unusual (Nowlis, 1969). Withdrawal symptoms have been reported in persons who took larger doses of barbiturates over an extended period of time and who became addicted as a result (Jenner, 1965). About one-fourth of deaths by poisoning diagnosed in general hospitals are the result of overdoses of barbiturates. An unknown number of these are suicides, but many are unintentional. These drugs are particularly dangerous taken in combination with alcohol (Ban, 1969). A number of other deaths, classified as automobile or other "accidents," may result from use of barbiturates.

In the youth drug culture, in which barbiturates and related drugs are known as "downers" and amphetamines and the like are called "uppers," some persons remain on a continual psychological roller coaster using one drug to counter the effects of another. This phenomenon occurs in many adults as well, but it is less well known because it is done in the home where it is less observable than among "street people." One writer compared studies of drug use in drug cultures, high schools, colleges, and among adults and estimated that the "up" and "down" drugs are used more frequently among adults on the whole, the "street people" being a small minority of young people (Smart, 1970).•

[2] "Deep sleep" refers to a state of dreamless sleep without rapid eye movements.

Psychotherapeutic Drugs

In addition to the noted popularly used drugs which are, more often than not, self-prescribed, we should mention the drugs which have been used with considerable success in the treatment of psychosis. The successful treatment of some types of schizophrenia with chlorpromazine in the mid-1950s led to intensive research in the use of drugs for mental illness (Thompson and Schuster, 1968). Although a given patient with particular symptoms may not respond in the same way as a similar patient with similar symptoms, one or another of the phenothiazine derivatives (of which chlorpromazine is one) has reduced aggression among mental patients. Such derivatives have also reduced the other symptoms enough that rehabilitation of many cases previously thought to be hopeless occurs routinely (Ban, 1969).

These and other drugs, since isolated and synthesized, have multiple effects on the nervous and hormonal systems. Reserpine, for example, isolated in 1956 from a plant "used in India for centuries for a variety of therapeutic purposes," also reduced tension and aggression and is known to reduce noradrenaline and adrenaline in the brain (Thompson and Schuster, 1968). However, because of its multiple effects on various body systems, the behavioral effect cannot be exclusively attributed to this particularly interesting biochemical phenomenon.[3]

The effects of drugs on depression are less spectacular than for some other types of psychosis. Up to 75 percent of depressed patients improve when given one of the antidepressant drugs, but up to 60 percent improve after they have had only placebos. Twenty to 25 percent of such patients recover with no drug therapy (Ban, 1969).

CONCLUSIONS

Even a cursory review of drugs and behavior illustrates the necessity for viewing behavior as the result of interactions of biological, social, and chemical phenomena. At the same time, one is frustrated by the complexity of these interactions and the difficulty of designing research which will reveal the particular combinations which result in particular behaviors. One veteran of such research has recently taken the pessimistic view that we may

[3] See the discussion of hormonal effects on behavior in Chapter 6.

never understand these patterns, particularly when researchers often study a drug to promote or discourage its use or use little imagination in designing their studies (Denber, 1970).

In addition to these problems, drugs taken under "natural" conditions are carried throughout the body and affect multiple subsystems. As a result, it usually is not possible to distinguish a particular biological mechanism or even a set of mechanisms which can be associated with psychological states or social behavior. It is sometimes possible to confine the action of a drug to a given site, but present technology for accomplishing this rules out the confounding effects of social settings or psychological states which prevail when the drug is routinely used. Nevertheless, this is no time to abandon the quest. Drug use of one form or another is a significant element of human behavior.

Suggested Reading

The basic issues of research and use of drugs for therapy are discussed by some of the most eminent thinkers in the field in Paul Talalay (ed.) *Drugs in Our Society* (The Johns Hopkins Press, Baltimore, 1964).

Thomas Ban's *Psychopharmacology* (Williams and Wilkins, Baltimore, 1969) is an excellent reference on the behavioral effects of particular drugs.

The Marihuana Papers (Bobbs-Merrill, New York, 1966) edited by David Solomon includes the original studies commissioned by Mayor La Guardia, commentary on marihuana use by literary and scientific figures, and a history of the legal status of the drug.

Two very different approaches to the investigation of opiate addiction are illustrated in Alfred R. Lindesmith, *Addiction and Opiates* (Aldine Publishing Co., Chicago, 1968) and in James R. Weeks, "Experimental narcotic addiction" (*Scientific American*, 210:46–52, 1964).

CHAPTER 10

CONCLUSION

MUCH IS STILL UNKNOWN ABOUT THE BIO-
logical aspects of human social behavior. However, the material
presented here should be sufficient to support our view that biological factors should be given more attention in theories and
investigations of social behavior. In this concluding chapter we
will suggest two lines of research—one focused on primates and
one on hormones—which appear to hold relatively high payoff in
knowledge to be gained relative to the ease with which the research
can be pursued. There are other areas, such as behavioral genetics
and the physical alteration of behavior through surgery and drugs,
in which the potential payoffs may be even higher, but methodological and ethical barriers in these areas are substantial.

PRIMATES

In Chapter 2, we compared the social behavior of several
primate species including *Homo sapiens*. Our method was analogous to the method of comparative anatomy, which compares
physical features across closely related primate species. We arranged primates into the following partial order: lemur, tarsier,
squirrel monkey, baboon and macaque, chimpanzee, and man.
There is an approximate progression in biological structure as we
move through this series, from lemur to man. Our intent was to
show that there is a similar progression in many forms of behavior. For example, the play of juvenile lemurs consists of stylized
locomotor activity with no object manipulation. As we move

through the primate series toward man, play becomes less stylized, complex games appear, and there is increasing object manipulation. We analyzed several other forms of behavior, such as mating periodicity and face-to-face interaction, in the same way. Our analysis of dominance and social-control behavior led to a major hypothesis of that chapter:

As we move up the primate series (from lemur to man), dominance-control systems become characterized less by overt "hands on" power behavior and more by subtle, normatively based deference-dominance behavior. The final stage of this trend appears in man; status and control in face-to-face groups is generally quite subtle, and physical agonistic attack within the group is very rare (Chapter 2).

In other words, the subtle normative means by which human beings maintain status and social control in face-to-face groups appears to be a characteristic of the species with a likely biological basis. We would expect to find it in any human group in any culture.

The primate series has some similarity to Mendeleev's periodic table of the chemical elements. Recall that Mendeleev was able to arrange all the known chemical elements into an orderly table, and in so doing he noted that several "vacancies" in his table must correspond to still undiscovered elements. From the positions of the vacancies in the table, he was able to guess the chemical properties of these elements. The missing elements were eventually discovered and Mendeleev's predictions were essentially correct. The primate series has several "vacancies," most notably for the tarsier, a primate which has not been studied in natural habitat. The placement of tarsier in the series, between lemur and squirrel monkey, allows a straightforward prediction of several aspects of tarsier behavior. We must await tarsier field studies to test these predictions.

A valid primate series would provide a useful method for studying certain questions about human beings which would otherwise be extremely difficult to research. For example, we have already discussed whether or not human beings are subject to the same sort of territorial instincts found in some other species. As we trace territoriality through the primate series, we find that evidence of such an instinct *diminishes* as we move from lemur to man. It would seem unlikely, then, that man has a biological basis for the protection of a territory. Other questions could be investigated using this logic. In Chapter 7 we showed how the primate series could be used to investigate human imprinting.

A variation of this research strategy derives from the Harlows' (1962) success in raising motherless baby macaques without any adult contact. The young macaques develop normally as long as they are allowed to play-interact every day. This suggests the feasibility of taking several infant macaques and raising them together with no adult contact, letting them mature, mate, give birth, and raise their own babies. We could, in effect, start primate societies from scratch to see how they develop with passing generations. Does a rudimentary culture develop? Are there regular changes in the social structure with passing generations? This would have to be a long-term study. A new generation of squirrel monkeys would come along every five or six years. Macaques would take somewhat longer, but lemurs would take less time. This sort of experiment ideally would be done in a more elaborate design. At least three species (say from the lemur, squirrel monkey, and macaque genera) would each be raised in two or more different types of seminatural environments. One environment might have plentiful food while another would have minimal food. To what extent would the differing ecologies be reflected in the developing societies, and how would these relationships vary as we moved up the primate series? We could test several current hypotheses which suggest that group size, social structure, reproductive behavior, and conflict level are functions of the availability of food. Preliminary results suggest how fruitful these experiments could be. Southwick (1969) observed agonistic interaction in a captive macaque colony while amounts of available food were varied. As expected, an increase in food supply resulted in decreased agonistic behavior; but, contrary to expectation, a decrease in the food supply also resulted in fewer agonistic interactions. There is much to be learned here.

A third type of experimental environment might also have minimal food supply but be equipped with various food caches which could be opened by using some ingenuity—e.g., pushing a lever, working a lock, using simple tools, floating a log "raft" across a water barrier. The purpose of this environment would be to encourage the development of a "technological" culture, and to the extent that it was successful, it would offer intriguing insights into the early development of human cultures just as Goodall's discovery that chimps make tools (Chapter 2) has jogged those theorists who have long considered tool making a purely human societal characteristic.

HORMONES

Two factors suggest that something of a "breakthrough" in social psychology may come in the next few years through our understanding of the relationships between hormones and behavior. First, the work of Funkenstein and Schachter (Chapter 6) demonstrates that hormonal responses to stressful situations are intimately related to social behavior in those situations. Second, unlike genetic factors which are extremely difficult to research, hormonal response can be measured and manipulated in the laboratory. Although our present picture of the hormone-behavior relationships is foggy, hopefully the picture can be cleared up shortly, thus giving us a new perspective on interpersonal behavior. We predict that within ten years a significant segment of social psychology will be centered around hormone studies.

Although the research is hardly begun, it is tempting to suggest some lines of inquiry based on the adrenaline and noradrenaline responses to stressors. The personality characteristic of *self esteem*, first brought into theoretical prominence by Alfred Adler and recently revived by Rosenberg (1965) and Coopersmith (1967), is a good place to start. Both recent investigators found a high correlation between self esteem and freedom from certain psychosomatic symptoms. These symptoms included hand trembling, heart beating hard, and shortness of breath, which are all associated with adrenaline reactions. This suggests that adrenaline plays a particularly salient role in the observable behavior of individuals with many psychosomatic symptoms (who also tend to have low self esteem), and so we hypothesize that these individuals—the low self esteem and high-symptom people—are more likely to have adrenaline responses to stress than noradrenaline responses. Adding Funkenstein's (Chapter 6, page 101) findings that adrenaline responders are more likely to show anger at themselves, or anxiety, than anger at others, we hypothesize that people with low self esteem are more likely to show anger at themselves, or anxiety, than anger at others. Although we are not aware of data which would directly test this hypothesis, Coopersmith does suggest that persons with low self esteem are more likely to vent their hostility toward inanimate objects (as opposed to people) than are persons with high self esteem. He reasons that those with low self esteem lack the assertiveness to be hostile to other people (Coopersmith, 1967:137–138). This string of variables is illustrated in Figure 10–1. It is easy, of course, to conjecture a feed-back loop from the tendency to be angry at oneself (or be anxious) to sustained low self esteem. This hypothetical scheme, should it have experimental validity, ties together personality, hormonal, and interpersonal variables.

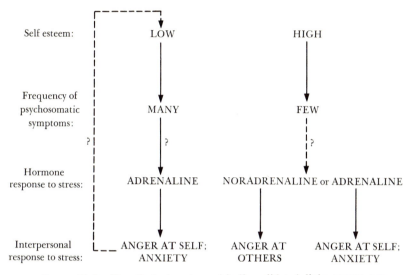

FIGURE 10–1.   Hypothetical and empirically validated links among personality, hormonal, and interpersonal variables.

What determines whether an individual customarily has an adrenaline or noradrenaline response to stress? There have been no twin studies or childhood socialization studies of this question. We do not know how stable the tendency to have one or another stress reaction is over an individual's life. Could hormone therapy aid in raising a person's self esteem, or could therapy directed toward raising self esteem alter the hormonal response?

Another potentially interesting line of research derives directly from Schachter's adrenaline experiments (Chapter 6). Recall that when he injected adrenaline into subjects who were not informed of the appropriate physiological symptoms to be expected from the hormone, the subjects had a relatively high tendency to show the emotion (euphoria or anger) of a stooge who was acting out these feelings. Schachter explained this effect by assuming that emotions are caused by two factors: a state of physiological arousal (such as is caused by adrenaline), and a cognitive "label" associated with that state. Presumably the aroused subjects who had no appropriate explanation, or "label," for their state of arousal, tended to label their arousal on the basis of cognitive clues from the stooge (Schachter and Singer, 1962). Whether or not that explanation is true, the adrenaline-uninformed (and misinformed) subjects did show a relatively high "sympathy" for the stooge. By sympathy, we mean that the subject tended to experience whatever emotion the stooge manifested—either euphoria or anger. This form of sympathy is ubiquitous in interpersonal behavior. When two people, ego and alter, are good friends, if alter feels euphoric, ego will also tend to be euphoric. But if ego dislikes alter, and alter is euphoric, we would expect ego to be unhappy rather than euphoric. Similarly, if the disliked alter is angry, ego should be rather pleased. What would happen, then, if Schachter's experiment were repeated with the additional feature that, through prearrangement or manipulation, the stooge was an enemy of the subject? Our guess is that the subjects, rather than sympathizing with the stooges, would antipathize—they would feel opposing emotions. If that indeed occurred, we would have demonstrated that the adrenaline-uninformed condition *caused* subjects to sympathize with friends and antipathize with enemies. It would then be tempting to interpret this condition, in which subjects feel symptoms which they cannot explain, as a *high stress* condition, relative to the adrenaline-informed, or low-stress, condition.

This is a tenuous line of reasoning which involves some conjecture, but if this picture were to emerge, we would have an excellent reason to look for hormonal effects in a large number of sociological phenomena which occur under stress. For example, the well-known tendency for coalitions to solidify during stressful conflict could be explainable as an adrenaline-intensified tendency to sympathize with friends while antipathizing with enemies. We would expect individuals who customarily respond to stress with a noradrenaline reaction to be less susceptible to this process than those who are adrenaline responders. Hysteric crowd behavior could be explained the same way, and, again, the noradrenaline responders should be less likely to be swept up. More interesting questions would be raised: Is the bond between mother and child the result of the stresses of early childhood? Or, to put it another (more researchable) way, do mothers of colicky babies sympathize more with their offspring than mothers of "good" babies who have placed relatively little stress on the family? Do married couples who spend their first year in bliss have less emotional bond (in later life) than couples who start their marriage in hardship? If so, are these all functions of hormonal responses to stress? And if so, do the noradrenaline responders show the same effects as the adrenaline responders? There are, we think, substantial possibilities for a social psychology which investigates hormone responses.

An adrenaline response could explain the hypothetical "critical period" when a child forms close affectional bonds to his parents and becomes fearful of strangers (Chapter 7). Stressful conditions are supposed to facilitate critical periods (Hess, 1962). Under this stress, adrenaline would intensify the child's tendency to sympathize with his familiar parents while at the same time antipathizing with strangers. If this mechanism is correct, we would expect autism to result from a malfunction of the child's adrenaline response system (or else from a lack of stressful events during the critical period).

We may be in for a highly practical payoff if the relationships between social interaction and hormonal reaction lead to techniques for the diagnosis and treatment of the stress-induced illnesses. It is known that some diseases are associated with hormone levels which are sustained outside their normal limits. The basic question underlying these findings is: What sustains these abnormal levels? A social stress theory of illness may provide the answer.

When a person who tends to need affiliation is socially isolated, he is stressed and his affiliation needs are amplified. If he is unable to find social interaction to satisfy the affiliation needs, he is stressed further and the cycle repeats itself with an accompanying sustained hormone level. A similar chain may occur for the nonaffiliative person; that is, stress increases the need to be alone, but the person's life situation demands intense social interaction which further increases his need to be alone, and so on. Should such a process continue, an illness may result depending on the hormones involved, genetic propensities, diet, and so on (Chapter 6).

The reader must certainly perceive that we are extremely optimistic about the potential payoffs, both theoretical and practical, which seem to await research into the various biological-sociological questions which are now open. We think, though, that our own level of enthusiasm is about as high as one can reasonably

go, and so our last word is to those whose enthusiasm sur-
passes ours.

A FINAL WORD TO THE OVERZEALOUS
CONCERNING EXPLANATIONS BY ANALOGY

Some theorists believe that several of our better-known large-
scale social phenomena—war, crime, social classes—can be explained as the result of man's biological instincts. They reason by
analogy: Fish protect territories by agonistic behavior against
their fellows; therefore (by analogy), human wars over territory
have a biological basis. Primate societies are always stratified so
that some individuals have more power and privilege than others.
Therefore (by analogy) the stratification of human societies into
more or less distinct social classes must have a biological basis.
We can illustrate the difficulty with this sort of explanation by
following the reasoning through in some detail:

All mammals which have been studied, birds, and some fish
display dominance behavior. It would seem forced to assume that
human dominance is a special case which alone does not have
some biological basis. Species differ in their forms of dominance,
and learned factors modify the process. In human beings it is
clear that cultural expectations affect dominance behavior. If an
experimental group is composed of individuals who, by virtue of
their occupations or ethnicities, have different "prestige" in the
larger society, these differences will usually be reflected in the
ensuing formation of the group's dominance order. That is, an
experimental group composed of a doctor and a laborer will
quickly form tacit (if not explicit) expectations that the doctor
ranks higher in the group than the laborer (Torrance, 1955;
Berger et al., 1966). This dependence on learned expectations
does not alter the basic conclusion that dominance ordering per
se is a biological characteristic of the species *on the face-to-face
level of interaction.* To this point the reasoning is sound.

If we move away from the level of primary face-to-face groups
up to the level of large societies, the biological explanation becomes tenuous. The stratification system of a large society is in
many ways analogous to the dominance order in a small group,
and it is tempting to assume that if face-to-face dominance behavior is a species characteristic, large-scale social stratification
must also be a species characteristic. *But there is no biological*

justification for this sort of explanation by analogy. We have not generally observed macro social stratification in other species—only dominance in face-to-face interaction. There is no basis for generalizing from one level to another. There is a discontinuity between stratification in a small group, on one hand, and in a large society, on the other. They are not the same phenomenon measured on different scales.

In the same vein, if there is an innate tendency toward some degree of face-to-face aggression in some men, it would not itself account for the observed tendency of societies to go to war. Hand-to-hand fighting is not societal warfare. Behavior on the face-to-face level need have no analogy to behavior at the societal level. Because a man likes to fight his friends is no reason to assume he wants to go to war.[1] Wars are not analogous to fist fights, shouting matches, or shootouts. There is no known *biological* reason why nations cannot live in peace.

At their worst, the biological arguments claim not only that man is a killer by nature, but also that he is the only species that kills its own kind. This is incorrect. There are many reports of animal "murders" in and out of captivity (Cloudsley-Thompson, 1965:71–100). For example, of about 150 baboons introduced into a London zoo colony over a six-year period, 38 died in fights (Zuckerman, 1932:220–222). It is true that most agonistic inter-actions between animals do not result in fatal, or even serious, injury, but that is also true of face-to-face agonistic interactions in human beings. Neither of the authors have ever observed a human murder, but one of us (Mazur) was at the scene of a macaque murder in a well-established semi-free-ranging colony.[2] Since our observations of macaques are far fewer than of human beings, we suggest that the human murder rate is lower than the macaque murder rate.[3] We have come to think of murder as "common-

---

[1] For example, a study comparing soldiers who got into fights during basic training with soldiers who did not get into fights showed that the fighters were somewhat less likely to have the makings of effective combat soldiers than the nonfighters (R. Smith, 1970: Chapter 15).

[2] The murderer was an adult male who was a major challenger for the leadership of the colony. He badly wounded a juvenile, apparently in a dispute over a piece of food, and the youngster died shortly thereafter. Immediately following the attack, several of the colony's adults coalesced against the attacker, and he and they engaged in substantial threat and counterthreat behavior, but there was no more physical contact.

[3] The United States murder rate (for human beings) is fairly constant ranging from five to seven per 100,000 population (President's Commission on Law Enforcement and Administration of Justice, 1967).

place" because of its frequency in the movies and on television and because the mass media give such wide coverage when a particularly interesting murder does occur in the real world. Yet most of us live our lives without ever engaging in fatal combat. So, if we must follow the current fashion of assigning a biological "nature" to man, then let us call him a rather peaceful fellow with a sense of humor.

REFERENCES

Ambrose, J.
1963 "The concept of a critical period for the development of social responsiveness." In B. Foss (ed.), *Determinants of Infant Behavior*, II. London: Methuen, pp. 201–225.

Andrew, R.
1963 "Evolution of facial expression." *Science*, 142:1034–1041.

Angermeier, W. F., et al.
1968 "Dominance in monkeys: Effects of social change on performance and biochemistry." *Psychonomic Science*, 11:183–184.

Ardrey, R.
1961 *African Genesis*. New York: Atheneum.
1966 *The Territorial Imperative*. New York: Atheneum.

Babst, D. V., J. A. Inciardi, P. K. Raeder, Jr., and D. Negri
1969 "Driving records of heroin addicts." Research Report No. 1969-11, New York State Narcotic Addiction Control Commission and New York State Department of Motor Vehicles.

Back, K. W., and M. Bogdonoff
1964 "Plasma lipid responses to leadership, conformity, and deviation." In P. Leiderman and D. Shapiro (eds.), *Psychobiological Approaches to Social Behavior*, Stanford: Stanford University Press.

Baker, S. P., L. S. Robertson, and W. U. Spitz
1971 "Tattoos, alcohol, and violent death." *Journal of Forensic Sciences*, 16:219–225.

Baldwin, J.
1969 "The ontogeny of social behavior of squirrel monkeys (*Saimiri sciureus*) in a seminatural environment." *Folia Primatologica*, 11:35–79.

Ban, Thomas
1969   *Psychopharmacology*. Baltimore: The Williams and Wilkins Company.

Bandura, Albert, and Richard Walters
1963   *Social Learning and Personality Development*. New York: Holt, Rinehart and Winston.

Barber, Bernard
1967   *Drugs and Society*. New York: Russell Sage Foundation.

Barchas, P., and M. H. Fisek
1969   "Rhesus and freshmen; studies in status orders." ASA Meeting, San Francisco.

Barnett, S. A.
1955   "Competition among wild rats." *Nature*, pp. 175–176.

Barrabee, P.
1953   "Postlobotomy changes in social behavior: Interaction content analysis, affect and productivity and ward adjustment." In M. Greenblatt and H. C. Solomon (eds.), *Frontal Lobes and Schizophrenia*. New York: Springer.

Barrington, E. J. W.
1964   *Hormones and Evolution*. London: English Universities Press Ltd.

Bartlett, D., W. Hurley, C. Brand, and E. Poole
1968   "Chromosomes of male patients in a security prison." *Nature*, July 27, pp. 351–354.

Bayley, N.
1966   "Learning in adulthood: The role of intelligence." In H. Klausmeier and C. Harris (eds.), *Analyses of Concept Learning*. New York: Academic Press, pp. 117–138.

Beach, Frank (ed.)
1965   *Sex and Behavior*. New York: John Wiley.

Becker, Howard S.
1953   "Becoming a marihuana user." *American Journal of Sociology*, 59:235–242.
1967   "History, culture and subjective experience: An exploration of the social bases of drug induced experiences." *Journal of Health and Social Behavior*, 8:163–176.

Becker, H., and H. E. Barnes
1961   *Social Thought from Lore to Science*, 3rd ed. New York: Dover Publications, Inc.

Beecher, Henry K.
1964   "Quantitative effects of drugs on the mind." In Paul Talalay (ed.), *Drugs in Our Society*. Baltimore: The Johns Hopkins Press.

Berger, J., B. Cohen, and M. Zelditch
1966 "Status characteristics and expectation states." In J. Berger, M. Zelditch, Jr. and B. Anderson (eds.), *Sociological Theories in Progress,* vol. 1. Boston: Houghton Mifflin Company.

Berkowitz, Leonard
1968 "Impulse, aggression and the gun." *Psychology Today,* September, pp. 18–22.
1969 *Roots of Aggression.* New York: Atherton Press.

Birrell, J. H. W.
1965 "Blood alcohol levels in drunk drivers, drunk and disorderly subjects, and moderate social drinkers." *Medical Journal of Australia,* pp. 949–953.

Bishop, M. P., S. T. Elder, and R. G. Heath
1964 "Attempted control of operant behavior in man with intracranial self-stimulation." In R. G. Heath (ed.), *The Role of Pleasure in Behavior.* New York: Hoeber.

Bloomquist, E. R.
1968 *Marijuana.* Beverly Hills: Glencoe Press.

Blum, R. H., et al.
1969 *Society and Drugs.* San Francisco: Jossey-Bass.

Brace, C.
1967 *The Stages of Human Evolution.* Englewood Cliffs, N.J.: Prentice-Hall.

Brauer, R. W.
1965 "Irreversible changes." In O. G. Edholm and A. L. Bacharach (eds.), *The Physiology of Human Survival.* New York: Academic Press.

Brill, H.
1969 "Psychosurgery today." *Diseases of the Nervous System,* 30, Supplement:54–55.

Bronson, F. H., and B. E. Eleftheriou
1964 "Chronic physiological effects of fighting in mice." *General and Comparative Endocrinology,* 4:9–14.

Brown, J. H. U., and S. B. Barker
1966 *Basic Endocrinology,* 2nd ed. Philadelphia: F. A. Davis Company.

Buckley, W. (ed.)
1968 *Modern Systems Research for the Behavioral Scientist.* Chicago: Aldine.

Burt, C.
1966 "The genetic determination of differences in intelligence: A study of monozygotic twins reared together and apart." *British Journal of Psychology,* 57:137–153.

Buss, Arnold, and Edith Buss (eds.)
1969 *Theories of Schizophrenia.* New York: Atherton Press.

Byrne, D.
1968 "The effects of physical attractiveness, sex, and attitude similarity on interpersonal attraction." *Journal of Personality,* 36:259–271.

Cannon, W. B.
1932 *The Wisdom of the Body.* New York: Norton.

Carey, J. T., and J. Mandel
1968 "A San Francisco Bay area 'speed' scene." *Journal of Health and Social Behavior,* 9:164–174.

Carpenter, C.
1965 "The howlers of Barro Colorado Island." In I. DeVore (ed.), *Primate Behavior.* New York: Holt, Rinehart and Winston, pp. 250–291.

Cartwright, F. F.
1967 *The Development of Modern Surgery.* London: Barker.

Casey, M., L. Segall, D. Street, and C. Blank
1966 "Sex chromosome abnormalities in two state hospitals for patients requiring special security." *Nature* February 5, pp. 641–642.

Chatfield, P. O.
1953 "Comparative anatomy and physiology of the frontal lobes." In M. Greenblatt and H. C. Solomon (eds.), *Frontal Lobes and Schizophrenia.* New York: Springer.

Chein, I., D. L. Gerard, R. S. Lee, and E. Rosenfeld
1964 *The Road to H: Narcotics, Delinquency and Social Policy.* New York: Basic Books.

Child, I.
1950 "The relation of somatotype to self-ratings on Sheldon's temperamental traits." *Journal of Personality,* 18:440–453.

Clark, W. Le Gros
1959 *The Antecedents of Man,* Edinburgh: Edinburgh University Press.
1961 *History of the Primates.* Chicago: University of Chicago Press.

Clausen, J. A.
1967 "The organism and socialization." *Journal of Health and Social Behavior,* 8:243–252.

Clement, W. R., L. P. Solursh, and W. Van Ast
1970 "Abuse of amphetamine and amphetamine-like drugs." *Psychological Reports,* 26:343–354.

Clossen, C. C.
1897   "The hierarchy of European races." *American Journal of Sociology*, 3:314–327.

Cloudsley-Thompson, J.
1965   *Animal Conflict and Adaptation*, Chester Springs, Pa.: Dufour Editions.

Cobb, S.
1961   "Foreword." In D. E. Sheer (ed.), *Electrical Stimulation of the Brain*. Austin: University of Texas Press.

Cohen, Sidney
1968   "A quarter century of research with LSD." In J. Thomas Ungerleider (ed.), *The Problems and Prospects of LSD*. Springfield, Ill.: Charles C Thomas.

Coleman, J. S.
1963   *Adolescent Society*. New York: Free Press.
1964   *Introduction to Mathematical Sociology*. New York: Free Press, Inc.
1968   "The mathematical study of change." In H. M. Blalock and A. B. Blalock (eds.), *Methodology in Social Research*. New York: McGraw-Hill.

Coopersmith, S.
1967   *The Antecedents of Self-Esteem*. San Francisco: W. H. Freeman.

Corning, W., and R. Von Burg
1970   "Protozoan learning: A bibliography." *Journal of Biological Psychology*, 12:91–96.

Cortes, J., and F. Gatti
1965   "Physique and self-description of temperament." *Journal of Consulting Psychology*, 26:432–439.
1970   "Physique and propensity." *Psychology Today*, October, pp. 42–44, 82–84.

Count, E.
1958   "The biological basis of human sociality." *American Anthropologist*, 60, December, pp. 1049–85.

Courville, Cyril B.
1955   *Effects of Alcohol on the Nervous System of Man*. Los Angeles: San Lucas Press.

Crancer, Alfred, et al.
1969   "The effects of marihuana and alcohol on simulated driving performance." *Science*, 164:851–854.

Crancer, Alfred, and Dennis L. Quiring
1968   "Driving records of persons arrested for illegal drug use." State of Washington Department of Motor Vehicles.

Crow, J.
1969   "Genetic theories and influences: Comments on the value of diversity." *Harvard Educational Review*, Spring, pp. 301–309.

D'Andrade, Roy
1966   "Sex differences and cultural institutions." In E. Maccoby (ed.), *The Development of Sex Differences*. Stanford: Stanford University Press, pp. 178–204.

Dalton, K.
1959   "Menstruation and acute psychiatric illness." *British Medical Journal*, 1:148–149.

Dart, R.
1959   *Adventures with the Missing Link*. New York: Harper & Row.

Darwin, Charles
1965   *The Expression of the Emotions in Man and Animals*. Chicago: University of Chicago Press.

Delgado, J. M. R.
1964   "Free behavior and brain stimulation." *International Review of Neurobiology*, 6:349–449.
1969a   *Physical Control of the Mind*. New York: Harper & Row.
1969b   "Radio stimulation of the brain in primates and man." *Anesthesia and Analgesia*, 48:529–542.
1970   "ESB." *Psychology Today*, May.

Denber, Herman C. B.
1970   "Can psychopharmacology advance?" *Psychosomatics*, 11:85–89.

Denenberg, V. H., et al.
1970   "Programming life histories: Effects of stress in ontogeny upon emotional reactivity." *Merrill-Palmer Quarterly*, 16:109–116.

DeVore, I.
1965   *Primate Behavior: Field Studies of Monkeys and Apes*. New York: Holt, Rinehart and Winston.

Dilger, W.
1962   "The behavior of lovebirds." *Scientific American*, January, pp. 87–97.

Dimont, M.
1962   *Jews, God and History*. New York: New American Library.

Dobzhansky, T.
1962   *Mankind Evolving*. New Haven: Yale University Press.

Dohrenwend, B. S., and B. P. Dohrenwend
1966   "Stress situations, birth order, and psychological symptoms." *Journal of Abnormal Psychology*, 71:215–223.

Dollard, J., L. Doob, N. Miller, O. Mowrer, and R. Sears
1939   *Frustration and Aggression*. New Haven: Yale University Press.

Dubos, René
1964 "On the present limitations of drug research." In Paul Talalay (ed.), *Drugs in Our Society*. Baltimore: The Johns Hopkins Press.

DuMond, F.
1967 "Semi-free-ranging colonies of monkeys at Goulds Monkey Jungle." *International Zoo Yearbook*. London: Zoological Society of London.

DuMond, F., and T. Hutchinson
1967 "Squirrel monkey reproduction: The "fatted" male phenomenon and seasonal spermatogenesis." *Science*, 24:1467-70.

Dwyer, J., and J. Mayer
1968 "Psychological effects of variations in physical appearance during adolescence." *Adolescence*, 3:353-380.

Eckland, B.
1967 "Genetics and sociology: A reconsideration." *American Sociological Review*, 32, April, pp. 173-194.

Ehrlich, P., and R. Holm
1963 *The Process of Evolution*. New York: McGraw-Hill.

Eibl-Eibesfeldt, Irenäus
1968 "Ethological perspectives on primate studies." In P. Jay (ed.), *Primates: Studies in Adaptation and Variability*. New York: Holt, Rinehart and Winston, pp. 479-486.

Ellefson, J.
1968 "Territorial behavior in the common white-handed gibbon, *Hylobates lar Linn.*" In P. Jay (ed.), *Primates: Studies in Adaptation and Variability*. New York: Holt, Rinehart and Winston, pp. 180-200.

Ellinwood, E. H.
1967 "Amphetamine psychosis: I. Description of the individuals and process." *The Journal of Nervous and Mental Diseases*, 144: 273-283.

Ellwood, C. A.
1938 *The Story of Social Philosophy*. New York: Prentice-Hall, Inc.

Erlenmeyer-Kimling, L., and L. Jarvik
1963 "Genetics and intelligence: A review." *Science*, December, pp. 1477-1478.

Epstein, I.
1959 *Judaism*. Baltimore: Penguin.

Essman, W. B.
1968 "Differences in locomotor activity and brain serotonin metabolism in differentially housed mice." *Journal of Comparative and Physiological Psychology*, 66:244-246.

Eysenck, Hans, J. (ed.)
1963 *Experiments with Drugs.* Oxford: Pergamon Press.

Eysenck, Hans, J.
1967 *The Biological Basis of Personality.* Springfield, Ill.: Charles C Thomas.

Falconer, D.
1960 *Introduction to Quantitative Genetics.* Edinburgh: Oliver & Boyd.

Fisher, Duke D.
1968 "The chronic side effects from LSD." In J. Thomas Unger-leider (ed.), *The Problems and Prospects of LSD.* Springfield, Ill.: Charles C Thomas.

Fisher, R.
1965 "Marginal comments on Mendel's paper." In G. Mendel, *Experiments in Plant Hybridisation.* Edinburgh: Oliver & Boyd, pp. 52–58.

Forney, Robert B.
1967 "The combined effect of ethanol and other drugs." In Melvin L. Selyer, Paul W. Gikas, and Donald F. Huelke (eds.), *The Prevention of Highway Injury.* Ann Arbor: Highway Safety Research Institute.

Franks, Cyril M.
1967 "The use of alcohol in the investigation of drug-personality postulates." In Ruth Fox (ed.), *Alcoholism: Behavioral Research, Therapeutic Approaches.* New York: Springer.

Freeman, W., and J. W. Watts
1950 *Psychosurgery in the Treatment of Mental Disorders and Intractable Pain,* 2nd ed. Springfield, Ill.: Charles C Thomas.

Frisch, J.
1968 "Individual behavior and intertroop variability in Japanese macaques." In P. Jay (ed.), *Primates: Studies in Adaptation and Variability.* New York: Holt, Rinehart and Winston, pp. 243–252.

Frisch, R., and R. Revelle
1970 "Height and weight at menarche and a hypothesis of critical body weights and adolescent events." *Science,* 169:397–398.

Funkenstein, D. H., S. King, and M. Drolette
1957 *Mastery of Stress.* Cambridge: Harvard University Press.

Gallup, Gordon, Jr.
1970 "Chimpanzees: Self-recognition." *Science,* January 2, pp. 86–87.

Gardner, B., and R. A. Gardner
1969   "Teaching sign language to a chimpanzee." *Science,* August
        15, pp. 664–672.
1971   "Two-way communication with an infant chimpanzee." In
        A. Schrier and F. Stollnitz (eds.), *Behavior of Nonhuman Pri-
        mates,* vol. III. New York: Academic Press.

Garn, S.
1971   *Human Races.* Springfield, Ill.: Charles C Thomas.

Geller, Allen, and Maxwell Boas
1969   *The Drug Beat.* New York: Cowles Book Co., Inc.

Geschwind, N.
1970   "The organization of language and the brain." *Science,* 170:
        940–944.

Glueck, S., and E. Glueck
1956   *Physique and Delinquency.* New York: Harper & Row.

Goffman, E.
1963   *Stigma.* Englewood Cliffs, N.J.: Prentice-Hall.

Goldfarb, W.
1943   "The effects of early institutional care on adolescent person-
        ality." *Journal of Experimental Education,* 12:106–129.
1947   "Variations in adolescent adjustment of institutionally reared
        children." *American Journal of Orthopsychiatry,* 17:449–457.

Goodall, J.
1965   "Chimpanzees of the Gombe Stream Reserve." In I. DeVore,
        Primate Behavior. New York: Holt, Rinehart and Winston,
        pp. 425–473.

Gottesman, I.
1968   "Biogenetics of race and class." In M. Deutsch, I. Katz, and
        A. Jensen (eds.), *Social Class, Race, and Psychological Develop-
        ment.* New York: Holt, Rinehart and Winston, pp. 11–51.

Gould, J., M. Henery, and M. MacLeod
1970   "Communication of direction by the honey bee." *Science,*
        1969:544–554.

Goy, R.
1970   "Early hormonal influences on the development of sexual and
        sex-related behavior." In F. Schmitt, G. Quarton, T. Melne-
        chuck, and G. Adelman (eds.), *The Neurosciences: Second
        Study Program.* New York: Rockefeller University Press.

Gray, P.
1958   "Theory and evidence of imprinting in human infants." *Jour-
        nal of Psychology,* 46:155–166.

Greenblatt, M.
1959   "Relation between history, personality and family pattern and

behavior response after frontal lobe surgery." *American Journal of Psychiatry,* 116:193–202.

Greenblatt, M.
1953   "Plan of study." In M. Greenblatt and H. C. Solomon (eds.), *Frontal Lobes and Schizophrenia.* New York: Springer.

Greenblatt, M., and H. C. Solomon
1953a   "Relative therapeutic efficacy of several operations: Superiority of bimedial lobotomy." In M. Greenblatt and H. C. Solomon (eds.), *Frontal Lobes and Schizophrenia.* New York: Springer.
1953b   "Concerning a theory of frontal lobe functioning." In M. Greenblatt and H. C. Solomon (eds.), *Frontal Lobes and Schizophrenia.* New York: Springer.

Greenblatt, M., et al.
1953   "Left vs. right lobotomy and the issue of cerebral dominance." In M. Greenblatt and H. C. Solomon (eds.), *Frontal Lobes and Schizophrenia.* New York: Springer.

Grinker, R. E.
1967   *A History of Genetic Psychology,* New York: John Wiley.

Haddon, William, Jr., and Victoria A. Bradess
1959   "Alcohol in the single vehicle fatal accident, experience of Westchester County, New York." *Journal of the American Medical Association,* 169:1587–1593.

Haddon, William, Jr., et al.
1968   *1968 Alcohol and Highway Safety Report.* Washington: U.S. Government Printing Office.

Hall, C.
1941   "Temperament: A survey of animal studies." *Psychological Bulletin,* 38:909–943.

Hall, K., and I. DeVore
1965   "Baboon social behavior." In I. DeVore (ed.), *Primate Behavior.* New York: Holt, Rinehart and Winston, pp. 53–110.

Hamburg, D. A., et al.
1968   "Studies of distress in the menstrual cycle and postpartum period." In R. Michael (ed.), *Endocrinology and Human Behavior.* London: Oxford University Press.

Hampson, John
1965   "Determinants of psychosexual orientation," In F. Beach (ed.), *Sex and Behavior.* New York: John Wiley, pp. 108–132.

Harlow, Harry
1965   "Sexual behavior in the rhesus monkey," In F. Beach (ed.), *Sex and Behavior.* New York: John Wiley, pp. 234–259.

Harlow, H. F., and M. K. Harlow
1962 "Social deprivation in monkeys." *Scientific American,* 207:136–146.

Hayes, Cathy
1970 "A chimpanzee learns to talk." In R. Kuhlen and G. Thompson (eds.), *Psychological Studies of Human Development.* New York: Appleton-Century-Crofts, pp. 331–399.

Heath, R. G.
1964 "Pleasure response of human subjects to direct stimulation of the brain: Physiologic and psychodynamic considerations." In R. Heath (ed.), *The Role of Pleasure in Behavior.* New York: Hoeber.

Hess, E.
1959 "Imprinting." *Science,* 130:133–141.
1962 "Ethology." In R. Brown, E. Galanter, E. Hess, and G. Mandler, *New Directions in Psychology.* New York: Holt, Rinehart and Winston, pp. 157–266.

Heston, Leonard
1970 "The genetics of schizophrenic and schizoid disease." *Science,* January 16, pp. 249–256.

Hill, W. C.
1955 *Primates,* vol. 2, *Haplorhini: Tarsioidea.* Edinburgh: Edinburgh University Press.
1960 *Primates,* vol. 4, *Cebidae.* Edinburgh: Edinburgh University Press.

Himwich, H. E.
1962 "Emotional aspects of mind." In J. Scher (ed.), *Theories of the Mind.* New York: Free Press.

Hollister, Leo E.
1968 "Human pharmacology of lysergic acid diethylamide (LSD)." In Daniel H. Efron (ed.), *Psychopharmacology: A Review of Progress, 1957–1967.* Washington: Public Health Service Publication No. 1836.
1971 "Marihuana in man: Three years later." *Science,* 172:21–29.

Hook, E. B., and D. Kim
1971 "Height and antisocial behavior in XY and XYY boys." *Science,* 127:284–286.

Huntley, R.
1966 "Heritability of intelligence." In J. Meade and A. Parkes (eds.), *Genetic and Environmental Factors in Human Ability.* New York: Plenum Press, pp. 201–218.

Hutchings, D. E.
1963 "Early experience and its effects on later behavioral processes in rats." *Transactions of the New York Academy of Sciences,* 25:890–901.

Imanishi, K.
1963   "Social behavior in Japanese monkeys, *Macaca fuscata*." In C. Southwick, *Primate Social Behavior*. Princeton, N.J.: Van Nostrand, pp. 68–81.

Isbell, Harris
1966   "Medical aspects of opiate addition." In John A. O'Donnell and John C. Ball (eds.), *Narcotic Addiction*. New York: Harper & Row.

Israel, Yedy
1970   "Cellular effects of alcohol." *Quarterly Journal of Studies on Alcohol*, 31:293–316.

Jackson, E. F.
1962   "Status consistency and symptoms of stress." *American Sociological Review*, 27:469–480.

Jasper, H. H.
1961   "Implications for the neurological sciences." In D. E. Sheer (ed.), *Electrical Stimulation of the Brain*. Austin, Texas: University of Texas Press.

Jay, P. (ed.)
1968   *Primates: Studies in Adaptation and Variability*. New York: Holt, Rinehart and Winston.

Jenner, F. A.
1965   "Use of drugs in anxiety states." In J. Marks and C. M. B. Pare (eds.), *The Scientific Basis of Drug Therapy in Psychiatry*. Oxford: Pergamon Press.

Jensen, Arthur
1969   "How much can we boost IQ and scholastic achievement?" *Harvard Educational Review*, Winter, pp. 1–123.

Jolly, A.
1966   *Lemur Behavior: A Madagascar Field Study*. Chicago: University of Chicago Press.

Jones, M.
1957   "The later careers of boys who were early or late maturers." *Child Development*, 28:113–128.

Jones, M., and P. Mussen
1958   "Self-conceptions, motivations, and interpersonal attitudes of early- and late-maturing girls." *Child Development*, 29:491–501.

Kalinowsky, L. B., and P. H. Hoch
1952   *Shock Treatments, Psychosurgery and Other Somatic Treatments in Psychiatry*. New York: Grune and Stratton.

Kasl, S. V., et al.
1970 "Serum uric acid and cholesterol in achievement behavior and motivation." *Journal of the American Medical Association,* 213:1158–1164, 1291–1300.

Kendis, Joseph B.
1967 "The human body and alcohol." In David J. Pittman (ed.), *Alcoholism.* New York: Harper & Row.

Kesey, K.
1962 *One Flew Over the Cuckoo's Nest.* New York: Viking.

Kessler, Seymour, and Rudolf Moos
1970 "The XYY karyotype and criminality: A review." Mimeographed paper, Department of Psychiatry, Stanford University.

Kety, S. S.
1959 "Biochemical theories of schizophrenia." *Science,* 129:1528–1532, 1590–1596.

King, H. E.
1961 "Psychological effects of excitation in the limbic system." In D. E. Sheer (ed.), *Electrical Stimulation of the Brain.* Austin, Texas: University of Texas Press.

King, J. A., and B. E. Eleftheriou
1959 "Effects of early handling upon adult behavior in two subspecies of deermice, *Peromyscus Maniculatus.*" *Journal of Comparative Physiological Psychology,* 52:82–88.

Klüver, H.
1937 "Re-examination of implement-using behavior in a cebus monkey after an interval of three years." *Acta Psychologica,* 2:347–397.

Koch, H.
1966 *Twins and Twin Relations.* Chicago: University of Chicago Press.

Koford, C.
1963 "Group relations in an island colony of rhesus monkeys." In C. Southwick, *Primate Social Behavior.* Princeton, N.J.: Van Nostrand, pp. 136–152.

Kohlberg, Lawrence
1966 "A cognitive-developmental analysis of children's sex role concepts and attitudes." In E. Maccoby (ed.), *The Development of Sex Differences.* Stanford: Stanford University Press, pp. 82–173.

Köhler, W.
1927 *The Mentality of Apes,* 2nd ed. New York: Harcourt Brace Jovanovich.

Kosa, J., and L. S. Robertson
1969 "The social aspects of health and illness." In J. Kosa, et al.

(eds.), *Poverty and Health: A Sociological Analysis.* Cambridge: Harvard University Press.

Kramer, John C., V. S. Fischman, and D. C. Littlefield
1967 "Amphetamine abuse." *Journal of the American Medical Association,* 201:305–309.

Kretschmer, E.
1925 *Physique and Character.* New York: Harcourt Brace Jovanovich.

Kuhlen, R., and G. Thompson (eds.)
1970 *Psychological Studies of Human Development,* 3rd ed. New York: Appleton-Century-Crofts.

Lasker, G.
1969 "Human biological adaptability." *Science,* 166, December 19, pp. 1480–1486.

Lawrence, C. W., and J. R. Haynes
1970 "Epinephrine and norepinephrine effects on social dominance behavior." *Psychological Reports,* 27:195–198.

Lenneberg, Eric
1967 *Biological Foundations of Language.* New York: John Wiley.
1969 "On explaining language." *Science,* May 9, pp. 635–643.

Lenz, W.
1963 *Medical Genetics,* E. Lanzl (trans.). Chicago: University of Chicago Press.

Lerner, I.
1968 *Heredity, Evolution and Society.* San Francisco: W. H. Freeman.

Lerner, R.
1969 "The development of stereotyped expectancies of body build-behavior relations." *Child Development,* 40:137–141.

LeShan, L.
1966 "An emotional life history pattern associated with neoplastic disease." *Annals of the New York Academy of Sciences,* 125: 780–793.

Levine, S.
1960 "Stimulation in infancy." *Scientific American,* 202, May, pp. 81–86.
1971 "Stress and behavior." *Scientific American,* 224, January, pp. 26–31.

Levinson, D., et al.
1953 "The relation of frontal lobe surgery to intellectual and emotional functioning." In M. Greenblatt and H. Solomon (eds.), *Frontal Lobes and Schizophrenia.* New York: Springer.

Lilienfeld, A.
1969   *Epidemiology of Mongolism.* Baltimore: Johns Hopkins Press.

Lilly, John, and Alice Miller
1969   "Vocal exchanges between dolphins." In R. Zajonc (ed.), *Animal Social Psychology.* New York: John Wiley, pp. 200–206.

Lindesmith, Alfred R.
1968   *Addiction and Opiates.* Chicago: Aldine.

Lindzey, G.
1967   "Behavior and morphological variation." In J. Spuhler (ed.), *Genetic Diversity and Human Behavior.* Chicago: Aldine, pp. 227–240.

Lisansky, Edith S.
1967   "Clinical research in alcoholism and the use of psychological tests: A reevaluation." In Ruth Fox (ed.), *Alcoholism: Behavioral Research, Therapeutic Approaches.* New York: Springer.

Loizos, C.
1967   "Play behavior in higher primates: A review." In D. Morris (ed.), *Primate Ethology.* Chicago: Aldine, pp. 176–218.

Long, L. (ed.)
1969   *The World Almanac.* New York: Newspaper Enterprise Association.

Lorenz, K.
1966   *On Aggression.* New York: Harcourt Brace Jovanovich.

Lubs, H., and F. Ruddle
1970   "Chromosomal abnormalities in the human population: Estimation of rates based on New Haven newborn study." *Science,* July 31, pp. 495–497.

Maccoby, Eleanor (ed.)
1966   *The Development of Sex Differences.* Stanford: Stanford University Press.

Mark, V. H., et al.
1969   "Remote telemeter stimulation and recording from implanted temporal lobe electrodes." *Confinia Neurologica,* 31:86–93.

Marler, Peter
1965   "Communication in monkeys and apes." In I. DeVore (ed.), *Primate Behavior.* New York: Holt, Rinehart and Winston, pp. 544–584.

Marler, Peter, and Miwako Tamura
1969   "Culturally transmitted patterns of vocal behavior in sparrows." In R. Zajonc (ed.), *Animal Social Psychology.* New York: John Wiley, pp. 220–224.

Martindale, D.
1960   *The Nature and Types of Sociological Theory.* New York: Houghton Mifflin.

Mason, J. W.
1968a   "The scope of psychoendocrine research." *Psychosomatic Medicine,* 30:565–575.
1968b   "A review of psychoendocrine research on the pituitary-adrenal cortical system." *Psychosomatic Medicine,* 30:576–607.
1968c   "'Over-all' hormonal balance as a key to endocrine research." *Psychosomatic Medicine,* 30:791–808.

Mason, J. W., and J. V. Brady
1964   "The sensitivity of psychoendocrine systems to social and physical environment." In P. H. Leiderman and D. Shapiro, *Psychobiological Approaches to Social Behavior.* Stanford: Stanford University Press.

Mason, W.
1968   "Use of space by callicebus groups." In P. Jay (ed.), *Primates: Studies in Adaptation and Variability.* New York: Holt, Rinehart and Winston, pp. 200–216.

Masters, W., and V. Johnson
1966   *Human Sexual Response.* Boston: Little, Brown.

Mayr, E.
1970   "Evolution at the species level." In J. Moore (ed.), *Ideas in Evolution and Behavior.* Garden City, New York: The Natural History Press, pp. 313–325.

Mazur, A., and J. Baldwin
1968   "Social behavior of semi-free-ranging white-lipped tamarins." *Psychological Reports,* 22:441–442.

McCall, R.
1970   "Intelligence quotient pattern over age: Comparisons among siblings and parent-child pairs." *Science,* 170:644–647.

McCarroll, James R., and William Haddon, Jr.
1962   "A controlled study of fatal automobile accidents in New York City." *Journal of Chronic Diseases,* 15:811–826.

Means, R. L.
1967   "Sociology, biology, and the analysis of social problems." *Social Problems,* 15:200–212.

Mechoulam, Raphael, Arnon Shani, Habib Edery, and Yona Grunfeld
1970   "Chemical basis of hashish activity." *Science,* 169:611–612.

Meduna, L. V.
1938   "General discussion of the cardiazol therapy." *American Journal of Psychiatry,* 94: Supplement, 40–50.

Mendelson J.
1969   "Lateral hypothalamic stimulation: Inhibition of aversive

effects by feeding, drinking and gnawing." *Science,* 166:1431–1433.

Michael, R. P.
1968   "Gonadal hormones and the control of primate behavior." In R. P. Michael (ed.), *Endocrinology and Human Behavior.* London: Oxford University Press.

Milgram, Stanley
1963   "Behavioral study of obedience." *Journal of Abnormal and Social Psychology,* pp. 371–378.

Mischel, Walter
1966   "A social learning view of sex differences in behavior." In E. Maccoby (ed.), *The Development of Sex Differences.* Stanford: Stanford University Press, pp. 56–81.

Mitscherlich, A., and F. Mielka
1949   *Doctors of Infamy: The Story of the Nazi Medical Crimes.* New York: Henry Shuman.

Mittwoch, Ursula
1967   *Sex Chromosomes.* New York: Academic Press.

Money, J., and A. A. Ehrhardt
1968   "Prenatal hormonal exposure: Possible effects on behavior in man." In R. P. Michael (ed.), *Endocrinology and Human Behavior.* London: Oxford University Press.

Montagu, Ashley
1968a "Chromosomes and crime." *Psychology Today,* October, pp. 42–49.

Montagu, Ashley (ed.)
1968b *Man and Aggression.* New York: Oxford University Press.

Morgan, C. T.
1965   *Physiological Psychology,* 3rd ed. New York: McGraw-Hill, Inc.

Morgan, G., and H. Riccuiti
1969   "Infant's responses to strangers during the first year." In B. Foss (ed.), *Determinants of Infant Behavior,* IV. London: Methuen.

Morris, D.
1967   *The Naked Ape.* New York: McGraw-Hill.

Moses
c. 1300 B.C.   Pentateuch.

Mourant, A.
1959   "The blood groups of Jews." *The Jewish Journal of Sociology,* December, pp. 155–176.

Mourant, A., and I. Watkin
1952   "Blood groups, anthropology, and language in Wales and the western countries." *Heredity,* 6:13–36.

Muhlbock, O., and L. M. Boot
1960 "Natural factors influencing host responses." *National Cancer Institute Monographs,* 4:129–140.

Mussen, Paul, John Conger, and Jerome Kagan
1963 *Child Development and Personality,* 2nd ed. New York: Harper & Row.

Mussen, P., and M. Jones
1957 "Self conceptions, motivations, and interpersonal attitudes of late and early maturing boys." *Child Development,* 28:243–256.

Napier, J., and P. Napier
1967 *A Handbook of Living Primates.* London: Academic Press.

Nash, Harvey
1962 *Alcohol and Caffeine.* Springfield, Ill.: Charles C Thomas.

Neel, J., and R. Post
1963 "Transitory 'positive' selection for color-blindness?" *Eugenics Quarterly,* 10:33–35.

Neilson, R. A.
1965 *Alcohol Involvement in Fatal Motor Vehicle Accidents in Twenty-seven California Counties in 1964.* San Francisco: California Traffic Safety Foundation.

Newman, H., F. Freeman, and K. Holzinger
1937 *Twins: A Study of Heredity and Environment.* Chicago: University of Chicago Press.

Nishida, T.
1970 "Social behavior and relationship among wild chimpanzees of the Mahali Mountains." *Primates,* 11:47–87.

Noback, Charles R., and William Montagna (eds.)
1970 *The Primate Brain.* New York: Appleton-Century-Crofts.

Nottebohm, F.
1970 "Ontogeny of birdsong." *Science,* 167:950–956.

Nowlis, Helen H.
1969 *Drugs on the College Campus.* Garden City, N.Y.: Doubleday & Co., Inc.

Ogburn, W., and W. Bose
1959 "On the trail of the wolf children." *Genetic Psychology Monographs,* 60: 117–193.

Ogden, C. K., and I. A. Richards
1959 *The Meaning of Meaning.* New York: Harcourt Brace Jovanovich.

Olds, J.
1960 "Differentiation of reward systems in the brain by self-stimulation techniques." In E. Ramsey and O'Doherty (eds.), *Electrical Studies on the Unanesthetized Brain*. New York: Hoeber.

Opler, M. E.
1945 "The bio-social basis of thought in the Third Reich." *American Sociological Review*, 10:776–785.

Park, R. E.
1931 "Mentality of racial hybrids." *American Journal of Sociology*, 36:534–551.

Parkes, J.
1964 *A History of the Jewish People*. Baltimore: Penquin.

Partenen, J., K. Bruun, and T. Markkanen
1966 *Inheritance of Drinking Behavior*. Helsinki: The Finnish Foundation for Alcohol Studies.

Paterson, A. S.
1963 *Electrical and Drug Treatments in Psychiatry*. New York: Elsevier.

Pescor, Michael J.
1966 "Physician drug addicts." In John A. O'Donnell and John C. Ball (eds.), *Narcotic Addiction*. New York: Harper & Row.

Petter, J.
1965 "The lemurs of Madagascar." In I. DeVore (ed.), *Primate Behavior*. New York: Holt, Rinehart and Winston, pp. 292–319.

Ploog, D., and P. MacLean
1963 "Display of penile erection in squirrel monkey (*saimiri sciureus*)." *Animal Behavior*, January, pp. 32–39.

Polani, Paul
1969 "Abnormal sex chromosomes and mental disorder." *Nature*, August 16, pp. 680–686.

Post, R.
1962 "Population differences in red and green color vision deficiency: A review and a query on selection relaxation." *Eugenics Quarterly*, 91:131–146.
1963 "'Colorblindness' distribution in Britain, France and Japan: A review with notes on selection relaxation." *Eugenics Quarterly*, 10:110–118.

Premack, D.
1970 "The education of Sarah." *Psychology Today*, September, pp. 55–58.
1971 "Language in chimpanzee?" *Science*, 172:808–822.

President's Commission on Law Enforcement and Administration of Justice
1967   *The Challenge of Crime in a Free Society.* Washington: U.S. Government Printing Office.

Puzo, M.
1969   *The Godfather.* New York: Putnam.

Quarton, G. C., T. Melnechuk, and F. O. Schmitt (eds.)
1967   *The Neurosciences—A Study Program.* New York: The Rockefeller University Press.

Ralls, K.
1971   "Mammalian scent marking." *Science,* 171:443–449.

Razavi, Lawrence
1969   "Sex chromosomes, hand-prints and sexual behavior." Read at the American Association for the Advancement of Science meeting, Boston.

Reichlin, S.
1968   "Hypothalamic control of growth hormone secretion and response to stress." In R. Michael (ed.), *Endocrinology and Human Behavior.* London: Oxford University Press.

Reynolds, V.
1968   "Kinship and the family in monkeys, apes and man." *Man,* June, pp. 209–223.

Rheingold, Harriet, Jacob Gewirtz, and Helen Ross
1969   "Social conditioning of vocalizations in the infant." In D. Gelfand (ed.), *Social Learning in Childhood.* Belmont, Calif.: Wadsworth, pp. 115–124.

Robertson, L. S., and L. E. Dotson
1969   "Perceived parental expressivity, reaction to stress, and affiliation." *Journal of Personality and Social Psychology,* 12:229–234.

Rosenberg, M.
1965   *Society and the Adolescent Self-Image.* Princeton, N.J.: Princeton University Press.

Ross, E. A.
1924   *The Outlines of Sociology.* New York: The Century Co.

Ruchames, L. (ed.)
1969   *Racial Thought in America.* Amherst: University of Massachusetts Press.

Sade, D.
1967   "Determinants of dominance in a group of free-ranging rhesus monkeys." In S. Altmann, *Social Communication Among Primates.* Chicago: University of Chicago Press.

Sakel, M.
1938 "The nature and origin of the hypoglycemic treatment of psychoses." *American Journal of Psychiatry,* 94: Supplement, 24–39.

Sampson, C.
1965 "The study of ordinal position: Antecedents and outcomes." In B. Maher (ed.), *Progress in Experimental Personality Research.* New York: Academic Press, pp. 176–228.

Sanderson, I.
1957 *The Monkey Kingdom.* Garden City, N.Y.: Hanover.

Savory, T.
1970 "The mule." *Scientific American,* 223, December, pp. 102–109.

Scarr, S.
1968 "Environmental bias in twin studies." In S. Vandenberg (ed.), *Progress in Human Behavior Genetics.* Baltimore: Johns Hopkins Press, pp. 205–213.
1969 "Social introversion-extraversion as a heritable response." *Child Development,* 40, September, pp. 823–832.

Schachter, S.
1959 *The Psychology of Affiliation.* Stanford: Stanford University Press.
1964 "The interaction of cognitive and physiological determinants of emotional state." In P. H. Leiderman and D. Shapiro, *Psychobiological Approaches to Social Behavior.* Stanford: Stanford University Press.

Schachter, S., and J. Singer
1962 "Cognitive, social and physiological determinants of emotional state." *Psychological Review,* September, pp. 379–399.

Schaffer, H.
1963 "Some issues for research in the study of attachment behaviour." In B. Foss (ed.), *Determinants of Infant Behaviour,* II. London: Methuen, pp. 179–196.

Schaefer, T. et al.
1962 "Temperature change: The basic variable in the early handling phenomenon?" *Science,* 135:41–42.

Schmitt, F., G. Quarton, T. Melnechuk, and G. Adelman (eds.)
1970 *The Neurosciences: Second Study Program.* New York: Rockefeller University Press.

Schultz, A.
1969 *The Life of Primates.* New York: Universe Books.

Schwitzgebel, R. L.
1968 "Survey of electromechanical devices for behavior modification." *Psychological Bulletin,* 70:444–459.

Scott, J.
1962   "Critical periods in behavioral development." *Science*, 30, November, pp. 949–958.

Scott, J., and J. Fuller
1965   *Genetics and the Social Behavior of the Dog.* Chicago: University of Chicago Press.

Sears, Robert
1965   "Development of gender role." In F. Beach (ed.), *Sex and Behavior.* New York: John Wiley, pp. 133–159.

Sears, Robert, Eleanor Maccoby, and Harry Levin
1958   "The socialization of aggression." In E. Maccoby, T. Newcomb, and E. Hartley (eds.), *Readings in Social Psychology.* New York: Holt, Rinehart and Winston, pp. 350–359.

Selye, H.
1956   *The Stress of Life.* New York: McGraw-Hill.

Sheldon, W. H.
1940   *The Varieties of Human Physique: An Introduction to Constitutional Psychology.* New York: Harper & Row.
1942   *The Varieties of Temperament.* New York: Harper & Row.

Shields, J.
1962   *Monozygotic Twins Brought Up Apart and Brought Up Together.* London: Oxford University Press.

Simonds, P.
1965   "The bonnet macaque in South India." In I. DeVore, *Primate Behavior.* New York: Holt, Rinehart and Winston, pp. 175–196.

Skeels, H.
1966   "Adult status of children with contrasting early life experiences." *Monographs of the Society for Research in Child Development,* Serial number 105.

Skipper, J. Jr., and C. McCaghy
1970   "Stripteasers: The anatomy and career contingencies of a deviant occupation." Case Western Reserve Sociology Department. Mimeographed.

Skodak, M., and H. Skeels
1949   "A final follow-up study of one hundred adopted children." *Journal of Genetic Psychology,* 75:85–125.

Smart, Reginald G.
1970   "Some current studies of psychoactive and hallucinogenic drug use." *Canadian Journal of Behavioral Science,* 2:232–245.

Smart, Reginald G., and Dianne Fejer
1969   "Illicit LSD users: their social backgrounds, drug use and psychopathology." *Journal of Health and Social Behavior,* 10:297–308.

Smith, C. U. M.
1970 *The Brain: Towards an Understanding.* New York: G. P. Putnam's Sons.

Smith, R.
1965 "A comparison of socioenvironmental factors in monozygotic and dizygotic twins, testing an assumption." In S. Vandenberg (ed.), *Methods and Goals in Human Behavioral Genetics.* New York: Academic Press, pp. 45–62.

Smith, Robert B.
1970 "Why Soldiers Fight." Sociology Department, University of California at Santa Barbara. Mimeographed.

Solomon, David (ed.)
1966 *The Marihuana Papers.* New York: The Bobbs-Merrill Co., Inc.

Southwick, C.
1963 *Primate Social Behavior.* Princeton, N.J.: Van Nostrand.
1969 "Aggressive behavior of rhesus monkeys in natural and captive groups." In S. Garattini and E. B. Sigg (eds.), *Aggressive Behavior.* Amsterdam: Excerpta Medica Foundation.

Southwick, C., M. Beg, and M. Siddiqi
1965 "Rhesus monkeys in North India." In I. DeVore, *Primate Behavior.* New York: Holt, Rinehart and Winston, pp. 111–159.

Sperry, R.
1964 "The great cerebral commissure." In *Psychobiology: The Biological Bases of Behavior.* San Francisco: W. H. Freeman, pp. 240–250.

Spitz, R.
1945 "Hospitalism: An inquiry into the genesis of psychiatric conditions in early childhood." *Psychoanalytic Study of the Child,* 1:53–74.

Spitz, R.
1965 *The First Year of Life.* New York: International Universities Press.

St. Laurent, Jacques, and James Olds
1967 "Alcohol and brain centers of positive reinforcement." In Ruth Fox (ed.), *Alcoholism: Behavioral Research, Therapeutic Approaches.* New York: Springer.

Staffieri, J.
1967 "A study of social stereotype of body image in children." *Journal of Personality and Social Psychology,* 7:101–104.

Stinchcombe, A. L.
1968 *Constructing Social Theories.* New York: Harcourt Brace Jovanovich.

Stott, Leland
1967 *Child Development.* New York: Holt, Rinehart and Winston.

Strongman, K., and C. Hart
1968 "Stereotyped reactions to body build." *Psychological Reports,* 23:1175–1178.

Thomas, W. I.
1897 "On a difference in the metabolism of the sexes." *American Journal of Sociology,* 3:31–63.

Thompson, T., and C. Schuster
1968 *Behavioral Pharmacology.* Englewood Cliffs, N.J.: Prentice-Hall, Inc.

Tiger, L.
1969 *Men in Groups.* New York: Random House.

Titmuss, Richard M.
1964 "Sociological and ethical aspects of therapeutics." In Paul Talalay (ed.), *Drugs in Our Society.* Baltimore: Johns Hopkins Press.

Torrance, E.
1955 "Some consequences of power differences on decision making in permanent and temporary three-man groups." In A. Hare, E. Borgotta, and R. Bales (eds.), *Small Groups.* New York: Knopf.

Tyron, R.
1940 "Genetic differences in maze learning ability in rats." *Yearbook of the National Society for the Study of Education,* 39:111–119.

Vaccarezza, J. R., et al.
1969 "The effect of stress on the urinary secretion of serotonin." *Review of Allergy,* 23:304–311.

Van den Berghe, H.
1970 "Nuclear sexing in a population of Congolese metropolitan newborns." *Science,* 169:1318–1320.

Van Lawick-Goodall, J.
1967a "Mother-offspring relations in free-ranging chimpanzees." In D. Morris, *Primate Ethology.* Chicago: Aldine, pp. 237–346.
1967b *My Friends the Wild Chimpanzees.* Washington, D.C.: National Geographic Society.
1968 "A preliminary report on expressive movements and communication in the Gombe Stream chimpanzees." In P. Jay (ed.), *Primates: Studies in Adaptation and Variability.* New York: Holt, Rinehart and Winston, pp. 313–374.

Vandenberg, S. (ed.)
1968 *Progress in Human Behavior Genetics.* Baltimore: Johns Hopkins University Press.

Wallace, George B., et al.
1966 "The marihuana problem in the city of New York." In D. Solomon (ed.), *The Marihuana Papers*. New York: The Bobbs-Merrill Co., Inc. (Originally published by Jaques Cattell, 1944).

Waller, Julian A.
1967 "Drinking drivers and driving drinkers—the need for multiple approaches to accidents involving alcohol." In Melvin L. Selzer, Paul W. Gikas, and Donald F. Huelke (eds.), *The Prevention of Highway Injury*. Ann Arbor, Mich.: Highway Safety Research Institute.

Wallich, H.
1970 "Population growth." *Newsweek,* June 29, p. 70.

Walster, E., V. Aronson, D. Abrahams, and L. Rottmann
1966 "Importance of physical attractiveness in dating behavior." *Journal of Personality and Social Psychology,* 4:508–516.

Ward, L. F.
1895 "Sociology and Biology." *American Journal of Sociology,* 1: 313–326.

Washburn, S., and I. DeVore
1963 "The social life of baboons." In C. Southwick (ed.), *Primate Social Behavior*. Princeton, N.J.: Van Nostrand, pp. 98–113.

Washburn, S., and D. Hamburg
1965 "The implications of primate research." In I. DeVore (ed.), *Primate Behavior*. New York: Holt, Rinehart and Winston, pp. 607–622.

Weeks, James R.
1964 "Experimental narcotic addiction." *Scientific American,* 210, March, pp. 46–52.

Weisberg, P.
1967 "Social and nonsocial conditioning of infant vocalizations." In Y. Brackbill and G. Thompson (eds.), *Behavior in Infancy and Early Childhood*. New York: Free Press.

Welch, B., and A. Welch
1968 "Differential activation by restraint stress of a mechanism to conserve brain catecholamines and serotonin in mice differing in excitability." *Nature,* 218:575–576.

Wenner, Adrian
1964 "Sound communication in honeybees." In *Psychobiology: The Biological Bases of Behavior*. San Francisco: W. H. Freeman, pp. 24–31.

Wenner, Adrian, Patrick Wells, and F. Rohlf
1969 "An analysis of the waggle dance and recruitment in honey bees." In R. Zajonc (ed.), *Animal Social Psychology*. New York: John Wiley, pp. 178–200.

Weyl, N.
1966   *The Creative Elite in America.* Washington, D.C.: Public Affairs Press.

Wilde, G.
1964   "Inheritance of personality traits." *Acta Psychologica,* 22: 37–51.

Woolley, D. W.
1967   "Involvement of the hormone serotonin in emotion and mind." In D. Glass (ed.), *Neurophysiology and Emotion.* New York: Rockefeller University Press and Russell Sage Foundation.

Wright, S.
1969   *The Theory of Gene Frequencies,* vol. 2. Chicago: University of Chicago Press.

Young, W., R. Goy, and C. Phoenix
1964   "Hormones and sexual behavior." *Science,* 143:212–218.

Zajonc, Robert (ed.)
1969   *Animal Social Psychology.* New York: John Wiley.

Zubek, J. P.
1968   "Urinary excretion of adrenaline and noradrenaline during prolonged immobilization." *Journal of Abnormal Psychology,* 73:223–225.

Zuckerman, S.
1932   *The Social Life of Monkeys and Apes.* London: Kegan Paul, Trench, Trubner and Co.

INDEX